Lisbon

DIRECTIONS

WRITTEN AND RESEARCHED BY

Matthew Hancock

WITH ADDITIONAL ACCOUNTS BY

Amanda Tomlin and Joe Budd

ROUGH
GUIDES

NEW YORK • LONDON • DELHI
www.roughguides.com

Contents

Introduction to

Lisbon

◄ Pastéis de nata

Set across a series of hills overlooking the broad estuary of the Rio Tejo (River Tagus), Lisbon's stunning location and effortless beauty immediately strike most first-time visitors. It's an instantly likeable place, a big city, with a population of around two million, but one that remains human enough in pace and scale to be easily taken in over a long weekend.

Although one of the European Union's least expensive capitals, Lisbon was once one of the continent's wealthiest cities, controlling a maritime empire that stretched from Brazil in the west to Macau in the east. Many of this era's grandest buildings were destroyed in the Great Earthquake of 1755, and much of today's city dates from the late eighteenth and nineteenth centuries. These days, apart from

▲ Overview from Castelo de São Jorge

When to visit

Lisbon is comfortably warm from **April** to **October** (average daily temperature 20–28°C), with cooling Atlantic breezes making it less hot than Mediterranean cities on the same latitude. Most **Lisbon residents take** their **holidays** in **July** and **August** (27–28°C), which means that some shops, bars and restaurants close for the period and the local beaches are heaving. Lower temperatures of 22–26°C mean **September** and **October** are **good times to visit**, as is **June**, when the city enjoys its **main festivals**. Even in **mid-winter** it is **rarely cold** and, as **one of Europe's sunniest capitals**, the sun usually appears at some stage to light up the city.

its individual sights, the biggest attraction has to be its streetlife: nothing beats watching the city's comings and goings from a pavement café over a powerful *bica* coffee or Portuguese beer. Alongside the cobbled streets and crumbling mansions are countless cosmopolitan bars and restaurants, many of them influenced by the tastes of immigrants from Portugal's former colonies. The city's buoyant nightlife scene

▲ View across Praça dos Restauradores up to the castle

is just as eclectic, ranging from the traditional fado clubs of the Alfama district to glitzy venues playing African and Brazilian beats.

If you're fit enough to negotiate its hills, Lisbon is a great place to explore on foot: get off the beaten track and you'll find atmospheric neighbourhoods sheltering aromatic *pastelarias* (patisseries), traditional shops, and shuttered houses faced with beautiful azulejo tiles. Getting around by public transport can be fun in itself, too, whether you're cranking uphill on one of the city's ancient trams, riding a ferry across the breezy

◄ Café Suiça

Rio Tejo, or speeding across town on the underground metro, whose stations are decorated with adventurous contemporary art.

Should city life begin to pall, take the train out to the beautiful hilltop town of Sintra, northwest of Lisbon, whose lush wooded heights and royal palaces comprise a UNESCO World Heritage site. Alternatively, the lively beach towns of Estoril and Cascais are just half an hour away, with the best beaches lying south of the city, along the Costa da Caparica, where Atlantic breakers crash on miles of superb dune-backed sands. Further south still, the popular resort of Sesimbra sits at the edge of the craggy Arrábida nature reserve.

▲ Street performers

Lisbon
AT A GLANCE

BAIXA

The eighteenth-century grid of the lower town is enclosed by hills and linked to the surrounding districts by a network of cobbled streets. Its elegant squares, filled with cafés, buskers and hawkers, form the hub of central Lisbon's daily activity.

◄ Chiado

◄ Praça do Comércio

CHIADO AND CAIS DO SODRÉ

Immediately west of Baixa, Lisbon's most elegant shopping area rubs shoulders with the more down-to-earth riverside district of Cais do Sodré.

◄ Alfama

ALFAMA

East of Baixa, this is the oldest, most traditional part of Lisbon, a village within a city, whose steep, whitewashed streets are so narrow that vehicles can barely enter. Overlooking it is a craggy hill topped by the leafy shell of the Castelo de São Jorge.

▲ Nightlife, Bairro Alto

BAIRRO ALTO

The upper town, northwest of Chiado, and best reached by one of the city's unique *elevadores* (funicular railways), shelters some of the city's best restaurants, bars and clubs. Further west, the redeveloped Alcântara docks is another nightlife hub.

BELÉM

West along the Tejo, this historic suburb, 6km from the centre, was where many of Portugal's great maritime explorers set sail to explore the new world. The turreted Torre de Belém has become Lisbon's most recognizable landmark.

FUNDAÇÃO CALOUSTE GULBENKIAN

North of the centre, this is an outstanding museum and cultural complex with an extraordinarily rich collection of ancient and modern art.

▲ Parque das Nações

PARQUE DAS NAÇÕES

Five kilometres east of the capital, this futuristic park occupies the former Expo 98 site, and has developed into a hugely popular riverside theme-park, with Europe's second-largest oceanarium just one of its attractions.

▲ Torre de Belém

Ideas

The big six sights

Lisbon is not known for one particular sight, but boasts a range of must-see attractions from the ultra-modern Oceanarium to the ancient Alfama district. All are within thirty minutes of the centre, which means you can comfortably visit all six sights in a long weekend – and as the cost of living is one of the lowest in the EU, the entry fees will barely dent even the tightest budget.

▲ Alfama

Lisbon's village in the heart of the city, a higgledy-piggledy maze of steps and tortuous alleys where life continues much as it has for centuries.

P.68 ▸ BACKSTREET IN ALFAMA

▲ Castelo de São Jorge

Originally a Moorish castle and later a palace and prison, the ruined castelo is now a tranquil haven with a bird's-eye view of the city.

P.74 ▸ CASTELO, MOURARIA AND GRAÇA

◀ Oceanário de Lisboa

Europe's most spectacular oceanarium, with a massive high-tech central tank containing all forms of sea life, from sea otters to sharks.

P.138 ▸ PARQUE DAS NAÇÕES

▼ Mosteiro dos Jerónimos

A monastery built to commemorate Vasco da Gama's discovery of a sea route to India, with flamboyant Manueline architectural features.

P.114 ▸ BELÉM

▲ Fundação Calouste Gulbenkian

From Ancient Egyptian to René Lalique; one man's astonishing private art collection housed in a stylish cultural centre.

P.127 ▸ PARQUE EDUARDO VII AND THE GULBENKIAN

◀ Torre de Belém

A superb example of the Manueline style, this ornate tower was built to defend the mouth of the Tejo river and has become the tourist board's icon for Lisbon.

P.118 ▸ BELÉM

Get moving

Lisbon differs from most cities in that getting around really is half the fun. With some of the steepest urban gradients in Europe, the city has developed a fleet of funicular railways and street lifts that crank up and down some of its back-breaking hills. Most of the funiculars date back to the nineteenth century or early 1900s, as do the wonderful trams whose routes skirt the central areas. Getting out of the city is also enjoyable, either by taking the train to Cascais or by crossing over the broad Tejo estuary on a ferry.

▲ Elevador da Bica

The city's most atmospheric funicular, starting under a hidden arch and gliding up a precipitous residential street.

P.84 ▶ CAIS DO SODRÉ AND CHIADO

▲ Elevador da Santa Justa

Lisbon's answer to the Eiffel Tower, a giant street-lift whose iron latticework dominates this section of the Baixa district.

P.53 ▶ THE BAIXA

▲ Trams

Lisbon's five remaining tram routes are
worth taking for the ride alone, and
fortunately all the trams ply useful routes
for tourists.

P.183 ▶ ESSENTIALS

▶ The ferry to Cacilhas

Take the short, blustery commuter ferry-ride
to Cacilhas from Cais do Sodré across the
Tejo for great views back over the city.

P.160 ▶ SOUTH OF THE TEJO

▼ Linha de Cascais

The spectacular train-line from Cais do Sodré
hugs the contours of the Tejo on the way to
Cascais coast, at times coming so close to
the water that waves splash the tracks.

P.153 ▶ CASCAIS COAST

Lisbon viewpoints

Old Lisbon's houses and churches are tightly packed across a series of hills facing the Tejo. At times it is easy to forget what a beautiful natural position the city occupies, and then suddenly a glimpse of a staggering vista is revealed between two buildings or down a steep street. The best views, however, are to be had from strategically placed *miradouros*, or viewpoints, usually frequented by the elderly for animated games of cards or dominoes, and the latest gossip.

▲ Elevador de Santa Justa

Not for vertigo sufferers, but ideal for a hawk's-eye view of the old town and the river.

P.53 ▸ THE BAIXA

▼ Miradouro de Santa Luzia

The best place to see over the terracotta rooftops of the Alfama and the eastern riverfront.

P.69 ▸ THE ALFAMA AND THE RIVERFRONT

▶ Miradouro de São Pedro de Alcântara

A broad, tree-lined viewpoint from where you can gaze down on the Baixa and the castle opposite.

P.90 ▸ THE BAIRRO ALTO

◀ Miradouro de Santa Catarina

Tucked-away *miradouro* offering dazzling views of the western riverfront. A popular hang-out for Lisbon's alternative crowd.

P.84 ▸ CAIS DO SODRÉ AND CHIADO

▼ Parque Eduardo VII

The top of the park offers an exhilarating panorama encompassing Lisbon and beyond, as far as the hills of Arrábida.

P.127 ▸ PARQUE EDUARDO VII AND THE GULBENKIAN

▼ Castelo, Mouraria and Graca

The viewpoint on Lisbon's highest hill, from where you can admire the castle and survey the whole of the city.

P.76 ▸ THE ALFAMA AND THE RIVERFRONT

On the waterfront

The Tejo was the departure point for some of the world's greatest explorers. However, surprisingly for such a great maritime city, Lisbon's waterfront was largely neglected until the late twentieth century, when its crumbling warehouses and docks were given a complete makeover. Now the Tejo has become a focal point once more, with waterside clubs, cafés and restaurants offering great outdoor terraces facing the river, so wide at this point that it is known as the "Sea of Straw".

▲ Parque das Nações

The former Expo site has evolved into one of Lisbon's most popular waterside suburbs, with modern residential architecture, cafés, restaurants and attractions all boasting fantastic Tejo views.

P.136 ▶ PARQUE DAS NAÇÕES

▲ Cais do Sodré

Slightly down-at-heel ferry and train interchange with highly atmospheric riverside walks.

P.83 ▶ CAIS DO SODRÉ AND CHIADO

▲ Belém

Developed by Salazar during a wartime Expo, the suburb of Belém has enough museums and attractions to warrant a full day-trip.

P.114 ▶ BELÉM

◀ Praça do Comércio

Historic Lisbon's riverside heart, a beautiful arcaded square and once the site of the royal palace.

P.51 ▶ THE BAIXA

▼ Doca de Santo Amaro

An attractive marina towered over by the Ponte 25 de Abril, a lively place for a drink or meal at any time.

P.109 ▶ ALCÂNTARA AND THE RIVERFRONT

Historical Lisbon

Olisipo was the administrative capital of Roman Lusitania, but the city grew up under the Moors, who occupied the city from 711 to 1147. Afonso Henriques became Portugal's first king in 1143 and the Moors were driven out by ruthless Christian crusaders in 1147. Within 400 years, Lisbon had become an economic powerhouse thanks to its opening up of trading routes around the world, and sumptuous monuments and churches were erected as symbols of its wealth. However, its golden age ended with the 1755 earthquake, and most of today's older buildings were built in the late eighteenth and nineteenth centuries.

▲ Alfama

This was once the centre of Moorish Lisbon, named *alhama* (hot springs) after the waters that rose here.

P.68 ▸ THE ALFAMA AND THE RIVERFRONT

▲ Bica do Sapato

This represents the new wave of cutting-edge designer bars, clubs and restaurants that have made Lisbon super-cool over the last few years.

P.81 ▸ EASTERN LISBON

▶ Padrão dos Descobrimentos

Belém means "Bethlehem", and this angular concrete monument commemorates the birth of the journeys to the New World in the fifteen and sixteenth centuries.

P.118 ▸ BELÉM

◀ Ethnic Lisbon

The 1974 revolution promoted a huge influx of immigrants from Portugal's former colonies, and nowadays African and Brazilian culture permeates Lisbon life.

P.103 ▸ SÃO BENTO, SANTOS
ESTRELA AND LAPA

▼ The Baixa

Europe's first great example of Neoclassical urban planning, the downtown area was built over the rubble of Lisbon's calamitous earthquake.

P.51 ▸ THE BAIXA

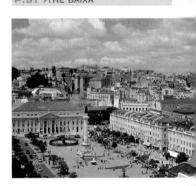

▼ Ponte 25 de Abril

Built in 1966, this towering suspension bridge was originally called Ponte de Salazar after the dictator who ruled the country with an iron fist for much of the twentieth century.

P.110 ▸ ALCÂNTARA AND THE
DOCKS

Lisbon museums

For a relatively small city, Lisbon has quite a plethora of museums. Many are of specialist interest or downright dull, but a few compare favourably to the best in the world. For around €3 a museum, you can enjoy many of Europe's finest paintings and sculptures and view some of Portugal's greatest artistic works throughout the ages. Lisbon is also gaining a reputation for contemporary art and design, with two excellent centres for modern art and its own design museum.

▲ Centro de Arte Moderna

Some stunning works of modern art from the best of Portugal such as Paula Rego, as well as an increasing British presence, including Anthony Gormley.

P.129 ▸ PARQUE EDUARDO VII AND THE GULBENKIAN

▼ Museu Calouste Gulbenkian

Virtually an A–Z of the history of art, from 4500-year-old Mesopotamian cylinder seals to the Impressionists, all set in a delightful park north of the centre.

P.128 ▸ BELÉM

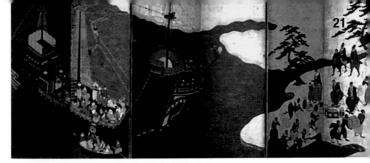

▲ Museu Nacional de Arte Antiga

Portugal's national gallery, with Japanese screens and sumptuous works by the likes of Nuno Gonçalves and Hieronymus Bosch, alongside applied arts from Portugal's former colonies.

P.105 ▸ SÃO BENTO, SANTOS ESTRELA AND LAPA

▶ Museu do Design

A history of modern design from the 1930s to the present day, taking in marshmallow chairs, kitsch designs and Philippe Starck pieces.

P.117 ▸ BELÉM

◀ Museu da Marinha

Lots about the Portuguese maritime explorations, battles and boats.

P.115 ▸ BELÉM

▶ Museu de Arte Moderna, Sintra

Small but richly stocked modern-art museum with a line-up featuring Gilbert and George, Jackson Pollock, David Hockney, Warhol and Jeff Koons.

P.145 ▸ SINTRA

On the tiles

Beautiful decorative tiles – azulejos – can be seen all over Lisbon, both inside and outside houses, churches, cafés and even metro stations. The word derives from the Arabic *al-zulecha*, "small stone", and the craft was brought to Iberia by the Moors in the eighth century. Changing technology and fashions have led to various styles of azulejo panels, including religious imagery, decorative tiled walls known as *tapetes* (rugs), Rococo designs and satirical portraits. Useful both for insulation and decoration, tiles continue to be used on buildings to this day, though most are now factory-produced imitations of the old hand-painted forms.

▲ Cervejaria da Trindade
Cavernous beer hall decorated with lovely nineteenth-century azulejos showing the elements and seasons.
P.94 ▸ THE BAIRRO ALTO

▼ São Vicente de Fora
The church cloisters contain superb early eighteenth-century azulejo panels, some illustrating the fables of La Fontaine.
P.79 ▸ EASTERN LISBON

▶ Museu Nacional do Azulejo

Fascinating museum tracing the development of the azulejo, set in the church and cloisters of Madre de Deus.

P.80 ▶ EASTERN LISBON

◀ The metro

Cais do Sodré is just one of many metro stations displaying adventurous contemporary azulejos.

P.83 ▶ CAIS DO SODRÉ AND CHIADO

▼ Rua da Trindade

A very Portuguese way to decorate your house: nineteenth-century tiles depicting science and progress.

P.90 ▶ THE BAIRRO ALTO

▼ Palácio dos Marquêses da Fronteira

This seventeenth-century palace is lavishly adorned with azulejos, including a whole room outlining scenes from the Restoration Wars with Spain.

P.133 ▶ NORTHERN LISBON

Churches and palaces

More money has been lavished on religious structures than almost anything else in the city and many of the solidly built churches withstood the devastating earthquake of 1755. As a result, today's churches are some of Lisbon's oldest and most rewarding places to visit, rich in architecture and azulejos tiles.

Other sumptuous buildings are the palaces, where Portugese royalty lived in opulent splendour until the Revolution in 1910. Little is left of Lisbon's main palaces at Castelo São Jorge and later Praça do Comércio, but numerous summer residences still remain.

▲ Mosteiro dos Jeronimós

Belém's monastery is considered one of the most beautiful in the country.

P.114 ▶ BELÉM AND AJUDA

▼ Convento do Carmo

Partly ruined in the 1755 earthquake, this fourteenth-century convent now houses the wonderfully eclectic Museu Arqueológico do Carmo.

P.92 ▶ THE BAIRRO ALTO

▶ Palácio Nacional, Sintra

One of Portugal's oldest and most beautiful palaces, built in the fourteenth century and containing classic Portuguese interior decor.

P.141 ▶ SINTRA

▼ Palácio da Ajuda

Construction of this palace was never completed, although that didn't stop its nineteenth-century royal tenants from kitting it out in extravagant style.

P.120 ▶ BELÉM

▲ Sé

Lisbon's cathedral is one of the city's oldest buildings, built in the twelfth century and sitting right alongside Lisbon's most picturesque tram route.

P.64 ▶ THE SÉ AND AROUND

▼ Palácio de Queluz

This elegant eighteenth-century palace is one of Portugal's greatest Rococo buildings, with extensive formal gardens.

P.151 ▶ SINTRA COAST, QUELUZ AND AROUND

Outdoor Lisbon

Lisbon does not have a surfeit of green spaces, so its parks and gardens are highly prized. Nearly all outdoor spaces have a café or kiosk of some sort to buy drinks and most have a play area for young children. All are abundant with rich semi-tropical foliage, making them ideal shady spots to escape the city heat. Take care in the larger parks after dark, however, when they can become the haunts of prostitutes and drug addicts.

▲ Parque das Nações

The former Expo site is one vast traffic-free area, embellished with trees, gardens and an extensive park stretching to the huge Vasco da Gama bridge.

P.136 ▶ PARQUE DAS NAÇÕES

▲ Praça do Príncipe Real

Not just a pretty space, this leafy square hides an underground water museum.

P.99 ▶ PRAÇA DO PRÍNCIPE REAL AND AROUND

▼ Jardim Botânico

Portuguese explorers introduced many plants to Europe from around the globe, and a fair proportion can be seen in these ten acres of hidden gardens containing around 15,000 species of plants and trees.

P.99 ▸ PRAÇA DO PRÍNCIPE REAL AND AROUND

▶ Parque Eduardo VII

Sloped, formal, city park edged with neat topiary shelters two cafés, hot houses and a couple of small lakes

P.127 ▸ PARQUE EDUARDO VII AND THE GULBENKIAN

▼ Jardim da Estrela

One of Lisbon's loveliest parks, with a lake, a band stand, and paths weaving through vibrant gardens and among towering palms.

P.103 ▸ SÃO BENTO, ESTRELA AND LAPA

▲ Praça das Amoreiras

Small but tranquil tree-shaded square bordered by the arches of the Águas Livres aqueduct.

P.124 ▸ AVENIDA DA LIBERDADE AND AROUND

Manueline to modern

The Portuguese have always used Europe's top architects for their grandest buildings: a Spaniard, João de Castilho, developed the Mosteiro dos Jerónimos in Belém; the Italian Felipe Terzi designed the church of São Vicente de Fora; and more recently the American Peter Chermaeff created the stunning Oceanário. Yet the most innovative architects have been the Portugese themselves: Diogo de Boitaca, for example, was the originator of the distinct sixteenth-century Manueline architecture, whilst today's world-renowned master is Álvaro Siza Viera has done much to reshape Lisbon's fire-damaged Chiado district.

▲ Eden building

Originally a cinema and now a hotel, this is the city's best example of Art Deco.

P.57 ▶ ROSSIO AND AROUND

▼ Palácio da Pena, Sintra

Disney-esque nineteenth-century palace high in the Sintra hills, whose furnishings remain untouched since the last royals fled in 1910.

P.144 ▶ SINTRA

▶ Torre de Belém

Considered the purest example of the Manueline style in Portugal, decorated with motifs representing Portugal's conquests abroad.

P.118 ▶ BELÉM

▼ Rossio station

Built in 1886, the mock-Manueline Rossio station entrance shows the enduring influence of this very Portuguese architectural style.

P.56 ▶ ROSSIO AND AROUND

▼ Pavilhão de Portugal

The Parque das Nações has countless examples of adventurous architecture, though Álvaro Siza Viera's sagging concrete roof on the Pavilhão de Portugal has the biggest wow factor.

P.136 ▶ PARQUE DAS NAÇÕES

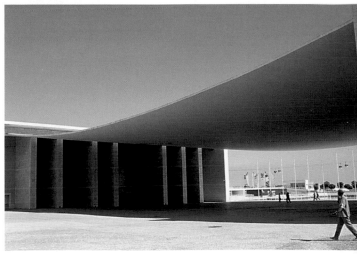

Weird structures

Partly because of Lisbon's geography and partly through sheer extravagance, the area around the city is well stocked with some fantastic and peculiar structures. Lisbon is built over seven hills facing an enormous river estuary – a taxing landscape for engineers – but they have overcome the problem with the construction of one of Europe's biggest aqueducts and one of its longest bridges. Throw in a bizarre hermitage and homages to wealth, Christ, and Freemasonry, and the weird and wonderful set is complete.

▲ Convento dos Capuchos

An extraordinary sixteenth-century hermitage carved from rock and cork in the wild hills above Sintra.

P.150 ▶ THE SINTRA COAST, QUELUZ AND AROUND

▲ Ponte Vasco da Gama

Built for Expo 98, and best seen from the Parque das Nações, the bridge stretches for 17km, 12km of it over the Tejo estuary.

P.136 ▶ PARQUE DAS NAÇÕES

▼ The Initiation Well, Quinta da Regaleira

Inspired by Freemasonry and hidden behind a revolving stone door, the spiral stairs, well and secret tunnel are straight from the pages of a fantasy novel.

P.145 ▸ SINTRA

▲ Mãe d'Água water cistern

The end of the line for the aqueduct is an eerily beautiful underground reservoir, now used for temporary exhibitions.

P.124 ▸ AVENIDA DA LIBERDADE AND AROUND

▶ Cristo Rei

Someone to watch over you: Portugal dictator Salazar's gift to the people, a mini version of Rio's statue of Christ.

P.160 ▸ SOUTH OF THE TEJO

▼ Aqueduto das Águas Livres

The amazing sixty-kilometre-long eighteenth-century aqueduct was once Lisbon's main source of water.

P.124 ▸ AVENIDA DA LIBERDADE AND AROUND

Lisbon hotels

Lisbon's hotel capacity is expanding every year, but it pays to book ahead to bag the best places. The least expensive options are good value, from €30 for a double room. For special occasions, €150-plus will get you a room in some of Europe's best hotels – and often for less if you go out of season. Lisbon's smartest areas are along the Avenida da Liberdade, around Parque Eduardo VII or in the prosperous suburb of Lapa. The most obvious places to try for inexpensive accommodation are around the main squares in the Baixa, and the streets Rua das Portas de Santo Antão and Rua da Glória, parallel to Avenida da Liberdade.

▲ Hotel Bairro Alto

Stylish hotel with a great rooftop bar – and an even better one on the ground floor.

P.171 ▸ ACCOMMODATION

▼ VIP Eden

Its self-catering apartments are nothing special, but the roof terrace and pool give this Art-Deco hotel the edge.

P.170 ▸ ACCOMMODATION

◀ Pensao Ninho das Águias

The views from this simple guest house make this one of the most popular budget options in the city.

P.171 ▸
ACCOMMODATION

▶ Residencial York House

Completely hidden from the street, this former convent has luxurious rooms and a lovely internal courtyard.

P.173 ▸ ACCOMMODATION

◀ Pestana Palace

Combining modern rooms with traditional opulence and fantastic gardens, this is rightly considered Lisbon's top hotel.

P.173 ▸ ACCOMMODATION

▶ Hotel Lisboa Regency Chiado

Designer hotel in the heart of the city, with superb views from its terrace and bar.

P.172 ▸ ACCOMMODATION

Dining out

Lisbon has some of the best-value restaurants of any European city, many serving food in traditional interiors that have barely changed since the nineteenth century. Unless you go to one of the many foreign restaurants, you'll find menus are fairly similar in content and price. You'll pay more for places in prime locations, with outside terraces or for superior service. Here is a selection of the best for all budgets.

▲ Bom Jardim, Rei dos Frangos

An unglamorous restaurant perhaps, but the best place in town for barbecue-grilled chicken.

P.61 ▸ ROSSIO AND AROUND

▶ Casa do Alentejo

Cross the tile-lined central courtyard to a
traditional upstairs dining room for solid
Portuguese food and Alentejan specialities.

P.61 ▶ ROSSIO AND AROUND

▲ Tavares Rico

An ornate eighteenth-century restaurant
replete with chandeliers, a favoured haunt of
Lisbon's business folk.

P.88 ▶ CAIS DO SODRÉ AND
CHIADO

▶ Cervejaria da Trindade

The nineteenth-century beer hall is touristy
but undeniably appealing, with decorative
tiles, a little garden and tasty seafood.

P.94 ▶ THE BAIRRO ALTO

◀ Rêsto do Chapitô

The menu may be limited
but the view is breathtaking and one of the best in
the city.

P.78 ▶ CASTELO,
MOURARIA AND
GRAÇA

Caffeine fixes

Lisbon has thousands of cafés, ranging from atmospheric, early twentieth-century artists' haunts and Art-Deco wonders to modern varieties with minimalist interiors. Lisboetas tend to head to a café or *pastelaria* (patisserie) for a breakfast of a croissant or pastry washed down with coffee – either a *bica* (espresso) or milky *galão* (a tall coffee in a glass). Cafés also serve snacks, drinks and even full meals. *Pastéis de bacalhau* (cod fishcakes), *rissóis de carne* (fried meat rissoles) and *pregos* (steak sandwiches) make great snacks, while Lisbon is famed for its *pastéis de nata* (custard tarts) and *bolos* (cakes).

▲ Antiga Confeitaria de Belém

This place serves the best *pastéis de nata* in Lisbon, though its cavernous interior is worth exploring in its own right.

P.120 ▸ BELÉM

▲ Café Versailles

Wonderful traditional café with waiters in bow ties and a fleet of coiffured women devouring cakes and sandwiches.

P.131 ▸ PARQUE EDUARDO VII AND THE GULBENKIAN

▼ Confeitaria Nacional

One of the city's oldest cafés, with great coffee and outdoor tables.

P.60 ▸ ROSSIO AND AROUND

▶ Suiça

Bustling café with counters groaning under the weight of cakes and pastries, and outdoor tables facing Lisbon's two main squares.

P.60 ▸ ROSSIO AND AROUND

▼ A Linha d'Água

Modern glass-fronted café with superb cakes, salads, and views of the park and lake.

P.131 ▸ PARQUE EDUARDO VII AND THE GULBENKIAN

▲ A Brasileira

The city's most famous café, opened in 1905 and the hub of café society ever since.

P.87 ▸ CAIS DO SODRÉ AND CHIADO

Lisbon bars

Portugal is rightly famed for its excellent wines and, though the locals rarely drink it in bars, you can always get a decent glass of *vinho* (wine) or *vinho do Porto* (port). Lisboetas are more likely to drink *cerveja* (beer), the two most common brands being Sagres and Superbock, either in *garrafas* (bottles) or draught: *uma caneca* is a pint; *um imperial* is a half. Local spirits are inexpensive and measures extremely generous. The local brandy, *maciera*, is smooth on the palate (but rough on the head). Even more lethal are the local *aguardente* firewaters, such as Bagaço or the cherry-based *ginginha*, which seem to fuel some workers from breakfast

▲ Lisbona

One of the most authentic local bars in the Bairro Alto, with good music for company.

P.96 ▸ BAIRRO ALTO

▼ A Ginginha

Tiny bar that's served *ginginha* since 1840: order it with or without the stone.

P.62 ▸ ROSSIO AND AROUND

▶ Solar do Vinho do Porto

This eighteenth-century former palace is the best place to sample port, including the underrated white variety.

P.97 ▸ BAIRRO ALTO

▼ Portas Largas

Ancient *tasca* (tavern) with original marble counter and tables, but a distinctly modern clientele.

P.96 ▸ BAIRRO ALTO

▲ Pavilhão Chinês

The "Chinese Pavilion" wins the award for quirkiest decor, and the cocktails aren't bad either.

P.102 ▸ PRAÇA DO PRÍNCIPE REAL AND AROUND

▼ Enoteca

Trendy wine bar with rooms in a cavernous former bathhouse.

P.102 ▸ PRAÇA DO PRÍNCIPE REAL AND AROUND

The Lisbon beat

No other sound encapsulates the mood of Lisbon so perfectly as fado, but Lisbon moves to a variety of other rhythms, especially those from its former colonies in Africa and Brazil. Jazz has a loyal following, while the classical-music scene is well represented at various venues and festivals. Lisbon's clubbing scene has a burgeoning reputation. The best place to head for a night out is the Bairro Alto, which from Thursday to Saturday becomes one big street party. Most places open around 11pm and few charge admission, though expect a "minimum consumption" policy, in which you pay on exit if you have not spent enough at the bar.

▲ Lux

Part-owned by John Malkovich and with a riverside terrace, this is Lisbon's top club; it also hosts concerts.

P.82 ▶ EASTERN LISBON

▼ Fragil

Enduringly trendy Bairro Alto style icon in a great old building.

P.96 ▶ THE BAIRRO ALTO

► B.leza

The best place to enjoy Lisbon's African music and culture.

P.107 ► SÃO BENTO, ESTRELA, SANTOS AND LAPA

◄ Hot Clube de Portugal

Small, sweaty, dark and laid-back: what more could you want from the city's best jazz club?

P.126 ► AVENIDA DA LIBERDADE AND AROUND

▼ Casas de Fado

There are countless fado houses, mostly in the Bairro Alto or Alfama; *Adega do Ribatejo* is a great place to start.

P.98 ► THE BAIRRO ALTO

▼ Bairro Alto bar-hopping

Head to the "high district" after midnight and you'll find Lisbon's heartbeat, with lively bars and clubs at every turn.

P.95 ► THE BAIRRO ALTO

Good buys

If you're used to characterless shopping malls, you'll find the Baixa's traditional and specialist shops refreshing. Even the city's shopping centres are quite an experience: families spend entire days out in them, eating all their meals, having an evening out at the cinema, and visiting a vast range of shops in between. Traditional shopping hours are Monday to Friday from around 9 or 10am to 7pm, with an hour or two's closing over lunchtime; most shops close Saturday afternoon. Larger shops are generally open all day Monday to Saturday, often until 10pm or later; some also open on Sunday. Many of the Bairro Alto's fashionable boutiques only open in the afternoon, from around 2 to 9pm.

▲ Espaço Fátima Lopes

Check out the latest designer clothing at this store belonging to Lisbon's queen of fashion.

P.93 ▸ THE BAIRRO ALTO

▲ Manuel Tavares

This traditional Baixa shop is a great place to buy port, wine, local cheese and confectionery.

P.60 ▸ ROSSIO AND AROUND

▼ Fábrica Sant'anna

A 250-year-old treasure trove of decorative tiles and ceramics.

P.86 ▶ CAIS DO SODRÉ AND CHIADO

▲ Mercado da Ribeira

Pungent and colourful food market, with regional crafts, food and cultural shows upstairs.

P.83 ▶ A CAIS DO SODRÉ AND CHIADO

▶ Feira da Ladra

Lisbon's best, most chaotic and atmospheric flea market can be visited on Tuesday and Saturday mornings.

P.79 ▶ EASTERN LISBON

▼ Armazéns do Chiado

Central Lisbon's most appealing shopping centre, with top-floor cafés offering fine city views.

P.85 ▶ CAIS DO SODRÉ AND CHIADO

Kids' Lisbon

The Portuguese are very family-oriented and children are welcomed everywhere. Hotels and pensions can provide extra beds or cots if notified in advance, usually free for under-sixes, while discounts on accommodation for older children can often be arranged. On public transport, under-fives travel free. Facilities for toddlers are less ideal. Changing facilities are scarce, as are high-chairs and menus specifically for children, though restaurants usually do half portions (ask for *uma meia dose*). Fresh milk is sold only in larger shops and supermarkets (most places sell UHT milk), though nappies, formula milk and baby food are widely available in supermarkets and pharmacies.

▲ Museu da Marioneta

From medieval marionettes to contemporary satirical puppets, this museum trumpets an art form that satisfied children long before the days of computer games.

P.106 ▸ SÃO BENTO, ESTRELA AND LAPA

▼ Museu do Brinquedo

This toy museum should fire the imagination of any child, and most adults too.

P.142 ▸ SINTRA

▶ Costa da Caparica

Lisbon's best beaches lie on the Costa da Caparica, where the quietest swaths of sand can be reached on a toy train.

P.161 ▶ SOUTH OF THE TEJO

◀ Parque das Nações

The perfect destination for families: traffic-free, with special children's play areas, international restaurants, an oceanarium, bowling and various other attractions.

P.136 ▶ PARQUE DAS NAÇÕES

▼ Dolphin watching

Leaping dolphins and the thrill of a boat ride make this a great day out.

P.164 ▶ SOUTH OF THE TEJO

▼ Sintra

With a toy train and horse and carriage, getting round this hilltop is always fun.

P.141 ▶ SINTRA

Day-trips

Though the city has enough attractions to keep visitors happy for days, it would be a shame to miss out on the beautiful and varied region around Lisbon. Most people are lured by the proximity of some superb Atlantic beaches, the best of which are south of the Tejo on the Costa da Caparica – though beware of fierce currents. Calmer waters are to be found west of Lisbon at Cascais and Estoril, or at the sheltered beaches around the Parque Natural da Arrábida further south. No visit to the area is complete without seeing Sintra, a mountain-top village where Portuguese royalty traditionally took their holidays.

▲ Cascais

Former fishing village turned resort, with some great beaches, a short ride from the capital.

P.153 ▶ CASCAIS AND ESTORIL

▼ Caparica

Favoured beach escape for Lisboetas, though fishermen still haul in drift-nets amongst the sun worshippers.

P.161 ▶ SOUTH OF THE TEJO

CASINO ESTO

◀ **Estoril**

Sandy beaches and a casino for those who want to indulge in a James Bond lifestyle.

▶ **Sintra**

See why Lord Byron proclaimed the village "in every aspect the most delightful in Europe".

▼ **Parque Natural da Arrábida**

It's worth the drive south to explore this rugged mountain range, whose dazzling white convent overlooks calm, sandy coves.

▼ **Cabo da Roca**

The most westerly point in mainland Europe, close to some wave-battered beaches.

Places

The Baixa

The tall, imposing buildings that make up the Baixa (Lower Town, pronounced bye-sha) house some of Lisbon's most interesting shops and cafés. Many of the streets are pedestrianized and, by day, they thrum with business folk and street entertainers. After dark, when the offices close, however, the whole area is strangely quiet. Facing the river, these streets felt the full force of the 1755 earthquake that destroyed much of what was then one of Europe's wealthiest capitals. The king's minister, the Marquês de Pombal, swiftly redesigned the sector with the grid pattern that is evident today. Pombal intended many of the grid's streets to take their names from the crafts and businesses carried out there, like Rua da Prata (Silversmiths' Street) and Rua dos Sapateiros (Cobblers' Street). Modern banks and offices have disturbed these divisions somewhat, though plenty of traditional stores remain; the central section of Rua da Conceição, for example, is still lined with shops selling beads and sequins. Other interesting streets to explore are the pedestrianized ones running south to north – Rua dos Correeiros, Rua dos Douradores and Rua dos Sapateiros.

Praça do Comércio

The beautiful, arcaded Praça do Comércio represents the climax of Pombal's design. Its classical buildings were once a royal palace and the square is centred on an exuberant bronze equestrian statue of Dom José, monarch during the earthquake and the period of the capital's rebuilding. Two of Portugal's last royals came to a sticky end in this square: in 1908 King Carlos I and his eldest son were shot dead here, clearing the way for the declaration of the Republic two years later.

Praça do Comércio's riverfront provides a natural focus for the area (when metro tunnelling is completed). In the hour or two before sunset people often linger the golden light to watch the orange ferries ply between the Estação Fluvial and Barreiro on the opposite side of the Tejo. The square is the starting point for tram and bus tours of the city (see p.184), as well as home

▼ PRAÇA DO COMÉRCIO ARCADES

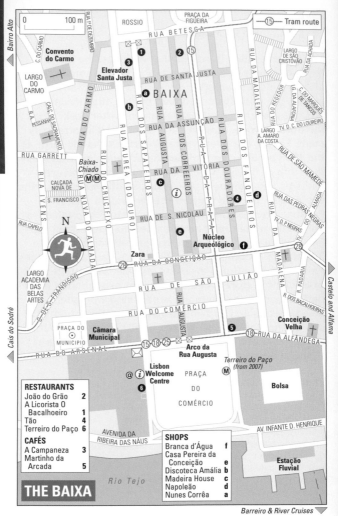

THE BAIXA

RESTAURANTS

João do Grão	2
A Licorista O	
Bacalhoeiro	1
Tão	4
Terreiro do Paço	6

CAFÉS

A Campaneza	3
Martinho da	
Arcada	5

SHOPS

Branca d'Água	f
Casa Pereira da	
Conceição	e
Discoteca Amália	b
Madeira House	c
Napoleão	d
Nunes Corrêa	a

Barreiro & River Cruises ▽

to the Lisbon Welcome Centre, the city's main tourist office (see p.182). It is also one of the main venues for the city's New Year's Eve firework festivities.

Praça do Município

The attractive, mosaic-paved Praça do Município houses the Neoclassical nineteenth-century Câmara Municipal (City Hall), where the Portuguese Republic was declared in 1910, flatteringly described by Portugal's greatest twentieth-century poet Pessoa as "one of the finest buildings in the city". The square adjoins Rua do Arsenal, an atmospheric street packed with pungent shops

selling dried cod and grocers
selling cheap wines, port and
brandies.

Arco da Rua Augusta and Rua Augusta

Praça do Comércio's most
prominent building is a huge
arch, the Arco da Rua Augusta,
adorned with statues of
historical figures, including the
Marquês de Pombal and Vasco
da Gama. The arch was built to
celebrate Lisbon's reconstruction
after the earthquake, although it
wasn't completed until 1873.
From here, the mosaic-paved
Rua Augusta is the Baixa's main
pedestrianized thoroughfare,
filled with shops, cafés, market
stalls and buskers.

Núcleo Arqueológico

Rua dos Correeiros 9 ☎ 213 211 700.
Advance bookings required. Thurs 3 &
5pm, Sat 10am, 11am, noon, 3pm,
4pm & 5pm; free.
The remains of Roman fish-
preserving tanks, a fifth-century
Christian burial place and
Moorish ceramics can all be
seen in the tiny Núcleo
Arqueológico, a museum
containing the remains of
excavations revealed during
building work on the BCP
bank. Most exhibits are viewed
through glass floors or from
cramped walkways under the
modern bank during a 30- to
45-minute tour. Pombal actually
rebuilt most of the Baixa on a
riverbed, and you can even see
the wooden piles driven into
the waterlogged soil to support
the buildings, the same device
that is used in Venice.

Elevador de Santa Justa

Rua de Santa Justa. Daily 9am–9pm.
€1.50. It is hard to avoid Raul
Mésnier's Elevador de Santa
Justa, one of the city's most

▲ STREET PERFORMERS ON RUA AUGUSTA

structures. Built in 1902 by a
disciple of Eiffel, its giant lift
whisks you 32m up the inside
of a straight latticework metal
tower, to deposit you on a
platform high above the Baixa.
Buy tickets at the booth above
the lower-level entrance. Before
taking the upper exit on to the
Largo do Carmo (see p.92),
head up the dizzy spiral staircase
to a pricey rooftop café with
great views over the city.

Shops

Branca d'Água

Rua da Conceição 28–30. Mon–Fri
10am–1pm & 3–7pm, Sat 10–1pm.
Fine small outlet for beautiful
hand-painted ceramics and tiles
in contemporary styles, along
with a few Portuguese
handicrafts. Recommended.

Casa Pereira da Conceição

Rua Augusta 102–104. Mon–Fri
9.40am–1pm & 3–7pm, Sat 9.40am–
1pm. Art Deco shop selling
tempting coffee beans, teas,
chocolates, cafetières, and china.
The aroma alone makes it worth
a visit.

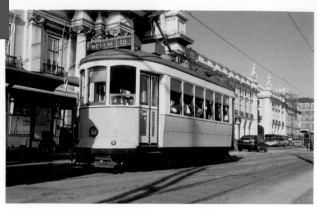

▲ TRAM IN PRAÇA DO COMÉRCIO

Discoteca Amália

Rua Aurea 272. Mon–Sat 9.30am–1pm & 2.30–7pm. A small but well-stocked shop with a good collection of traditional Portuguese fado music. If you're looking for a recommendation, the English-speaking staff are usually happy to help.

Madeira House

Rua Augusta 133. Mon–Sat 9am–2pm & 3–7pm. As you'd expect, linens and embroidery from Madeira feature, along with ceramics, tiles and souvenirs from the mainland.

Napoleão

Rua dos Fanqueiros 70. Mon–Sat 9.30am–8pm. This spruce shop offers a great range of quality port and wine from all Portugal's main regions, and its enthusiastic, English-speaking staff can advise on what to buy.

Nunes Corrêa

Rua Augusta 250. Mon–Sat 10am–7pm. Upmarket fashion store with a limited but quality range of shoes, leather jackets and jumpers, some with designer labels.

Cafés

A Campaneza

Rua dos Sapateiros 157. Mon–Sat 7am–8pm. Formerly a *leitaria* (dairy shop) and still displaying the decor from its past existence, this is now a simple *pastelaria* (pastry shop), with decent inexpensive snacks and coffee.

Martinho da Arcada

Praça do Comércio 3 ☎218 879 259. Mon–Sat noon–3pm & 7–11pm. One of Lisbon's oldest café-restaurants, first opened in 1782 and declared a national monument as long ago as 1910. Over the years it has been a gambling den, a meeting place for political dissidents and, later, a more reputable hangout for politicians, writers and artists. It is now divided into a simple stand-up café and a slightly pricey restaurant. The outdoor tables under the arches are a perfect spot for a coffee and a *pastel de nata* or a light lunch.

Restaurants

João do Grão
Rua dos Correeiros 220–228 ☎ 213 424 757. Daily noon–3.30pm & 6–11pm. One of the best in a row of restaurants on this pedestrianized street, where appealing outdoor tables tempt you to sit down and sample the reasonably priced Portuguese salads, fish and rice dishes. The marble- and azulejo-clad interior is just as attractive.

A Licorista O Bacalhoeiro
Rua dos Sapateiros 222–224 ☎ 213 431 415. Mon–Fri 8am–8pm, Sat 8am–1pm. This pleasant tile-and-brick restaurant is a popular lunchtime stop, when locals flock in for inexpensive set meals.

Tão
Rua dos Douradores 10 ☎ 218 850 046. Mon–Sat noon–3.30pm & 6.30–9.30pm. Fashionable, very good value eastern-inspired vegetarian restaurant, with set meals from around €5. Tasty vegetarian sushi, risottos, grilled aubergines and salads.

Terreiro do Paço
Praça do Comércio ☎ 210 312 850. Tues–Sat 12.30–3pm & 8pm–11pm, Sun 12.30–3pm. Expensive but stylish restaurant right on the square serving high-quality dishes such as caramelized duck or oyster mousse with pine nuts, accompanied by wine served in glasses the size of pumpkins. Downstairs tables are separated by wooden screens, though the nicest tables are in the cavernous, brick-vaulted upstairs room. Saturday lunch features a traditional serving of *cozido*, while Sunday brunch concentrates on Portuguese specialities – often including *bacalhau*. Reservations are advised for Sunday brunch and for dinner.

Rossio and around

Rossio has been the city's main square since medieval times and it remains the hub of commercial Lisbon, along with the adjacent squares Praça da Figueira, Largo Martim Moniz and Praça dos Restauradores. Bustling and noisy, this is where tourists new to the city find their feet, and is the area you're most likely to be offered a dodgy watch or "hasheesh". The squares are also important transport interchanges.

Rossio

Praça Dom Pedro IV (popularly known as Rossio) sparkles with Baroque fountains and polished, mosaic-cobbled pavements. During the nineteenth century, Rossio's plethora of cafés attracted Lisbon's painters and writers, though many of the artists' haunts were converted to banks in the 1970s. Nevertheless, the outdoor seats of the square's remaining cafés are perennially popular meeting points. On the northwestern side of the square, there's a horseshoe-shaped entrance to Rossio station, a mock-Manueline complex with the train platforms an escalator ride above the street-level entrances.

Teatro Nacional de Dona Maria II

☎ 213 472 246, ⊛ www.teatro-dmaria .pt. Rossio's biggest concession to grandeur is the Teatro Nacional de Dona Maria II built along its north side in the 1840s, and heavily restored after a fire in 1964. A statue of Gil Vicente, Portugal's sixteenth-century equivalent of Shakespeare, sits atop the facade, and inside there is a good café (see p.60). Prior to the earthquake, the Inquisitional Palace stood on this site, in front of which public hangings and autos-da-fé (ritual burnings of heretics) took place.

Igreja de São Domingos

The Igreja de São Domingos stands on the site of the thirteenth-century Convento de São Domingos, where sentences were read out during the Inquisition. The convent was destroyed in the earthquake of 1755, though its portal was reconstructed soon after as part of the current Dominican church, which was built on the same spot. For over a century it was the venue for royal marriages and christenings,

▼ ROSSIO STATION

▲ PRAÇA DOS RESTAURADORES

though it lost this role after the declaration of the Republic and was then gutted by a fire in the 1950s. It was reopened in 1997 after partial restoration to replace the seats and some statues; however, the rest of the cavernous interior and the scarred pillars remain powerfully atmospheric.

Praça da Figueira

Praça da Figueira is an historic square (once the site of Lisbon's main market), though the recent addition of an underground car park has detracted from its former grandeur. Nevertheless, it is slightly quieter than Rossio, and its cafés offer appealing views of the green slopes of the Castelo de São Jorge above.

Praça dos Restauradores

The elongated Praça dos Restauradores (Square of the Restorers) takes its name from the renewal of independence from Spain in 1640. To the north of the square, the **Elevador da Glória** offers access to the Bairro Alto (see p.90); south sits the superb Art Deco frontage of the old Eden cinema, now an apartment-hotel (see p.170) The square is dominated by the pink Palácio de Foz on the western side, which housed the Ministry of Propaganda under the Salazar regime (1932–74) but is now home to the Portuguese Tourist Office (see p.182) and tourist police station. During the week it is sometimes possible to visit the palace's ornate upper floors, resplendent with chandeliers; check in the tourist office for details.

Rua das Portas de Santo Antão

Rua das Portas de Santo Antão is the area's main pedestrianized drag, well-known for its seafood restaurants. Despite the tourist trappings – this and the adjacent Rua Jardim Regedor are the only places in town you're likely to get waiters trying to smooth-talk you into their premises – the street does have some fine local haunts. Providing you choose carefully, it is worth eating here at least once to sample its seafood, and to enjoy some of the city's best people-watching. The street is also home to several theatres

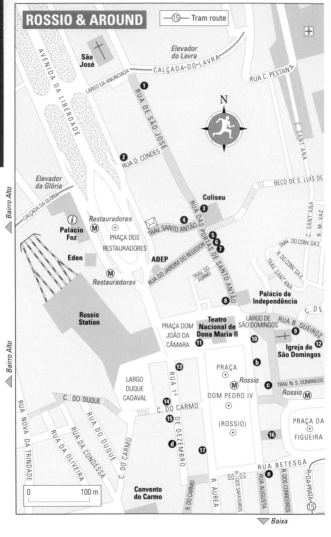

ROSSIO & AROUND ──⑮── Tram route

Bairro Alto

Bairro Alto

AVENIDA DA LIBERDADE

São José

Elevador do Lavra

CALÇADA DO LAVRA

RUA C. PESTANA

LARGO DA ANUNCIADA

RUA DE SÃO JOSÉ

N

C. SANT'ANA

❶

❷ RUA D. CONDES

Elevador da Glória

CALÇADA DA GLÓRIA

BECO DE S. LUÍS DE

Coliseu

RUA DAS PORTAS DE SANTO ANTÃO

❸
❹ TRAV. SANTO ANTÃO

C. SANT'ANA

C. SANT'ANA
R. M. VAZ

ⓘ Restauradores
Palácio Foz Ⓜ
⊙ PRAÇA DOS RESTAURADORES

❺
❻
❼

TRAV. DO CONV. DA E.
R. DO CONV. DA E.
TRAV. SANT'ANA

Eden ABEP

RUA DO JARDIM DO REGEDOR

TRAV. DO FORNO

❽

Palácio da Independência

Restauradores Ⓜ

Rossio Station

PRAÇA DOM JOÃO DA CÂMARA

Teatro Nacional de Dona Maria II
❶❶

LARGO DE SÃO DOMINGOS

RUA B. QUEIRÓZ
❾

C. DE

LARGO DUQUE CADAVAL

❶❸

RUA 1º DE DEZEMBRO

❶❹
❶❺
ⓓ

C. DO CARMO

❶❷
Igreja de São Domingos

PRAÇA
⊙
Rossio Ⓜ
DOM PEDRO IV

(ROSSIO)
⊙

❿
ⓑ

ⓒ TRAV. N. S. DOMINGOS
Rossio Ⓜ

PRAÇA DA
⊙
FIGUEIRA

C. DO DUQUE

RUA NOVA DA TRINDADE

RUA DA OLIVEIRA

RUA DA CONDESSA

RUA DO DUQUE

C. DO CARMO

❶❼

❶❻

RUA BETESGA
❽ R. DOS CORREEIROS

0   100 m

Convento do Carmo

R. DO CARMO
R. AUREA
R. DOS SAPATEIROS
RUA AUGUSTA
R. DA PRATA
⑮

▽ Baixa

and the domed **Coliseu dos Recreios** at #96 (☎213 240 580, ⓦ www.coliseulisboa.com) opened in 1890 as a circus but is now one of Lisbon's main concert venues.

Rua das Portas de Santo Antão ends next to where another of the city's classic *elevadores*,

Elevador do Lavra, begins its ascent (see p.122 for details).

Shops

Azevedo Rua Chapetaria

Rossio 6973. Traditional hats, berets, walking sticks, canes and

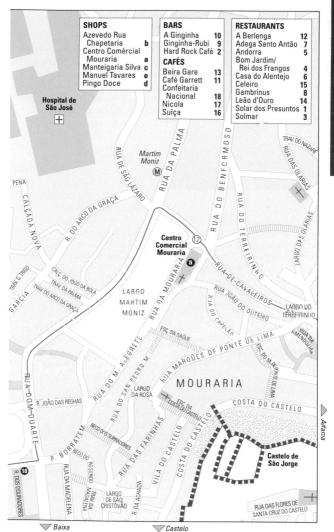

SHOPS	
Azevedo Rua Chapetaria	**b**
Centro Comércial Mouraria	**a**
Manteigaria Silva	**c**
Manuel Tavares	**e**
Pingo Doce	**d**

BARS	
A Ginginha	**10**
Ginginha-Rubi	**9**
Hard Rock Café	**2**
CAFÉS	
Beira Gare	**13**
Café Garrett	**11**
Confeitaria Nacional	
Nicola	**17**
Suíça	**16**

RESTAURANTS	
A Berlenga	**12**
Adega Santo Antão	**7**
Andorra	**5**
Bom Jardim/ Rei dos Frangos	**4**
Casa do Alentejo	**6**
Celeiro	**15**
Gambrinus	**8**
Leão d'Ouro	**14**
Solar dos Presuntos	**1**
Solmar	**3**

belts in a lovely wood-panelled shop.

Centro Comércial Mouraria

Largo Martim Moniz. Largo Martim Moniz formed the gateway to the medieval city and took its name from a Christian knight who died trying to keep the gates open during a crusade against the occupying Moors. Today's rather drab concrete expanse is enlivened by the city's tackiest and most run-down shopping centre, sufficiently atmospheric to warrant a look around its six levels (three of them

▲ AZEVEDO RUA HAT SHOP

underground). Hundreds of small, family-run stores selling Indian fabrics and Oriental and African produce, alongside an aromatic collection of cafés on Level −3, give a real insight into Lisbon's ethnic communities, perfect if you need an Afro haircut or a samosa.

Manteigaria Silva

Rua D. Antão de Almada 1. One of Lisbon's many pungent traditional delis, stocked with a tempting array of cured hams, dried fruits and nuts. The figs soaked in honey are superb.

Manuel Tavares

Rua da Betesga 1a. Small, century-old treasure-trove, with a great selection of nuts, chocolate and national cheeses, and a basement stuffed with vintage wines and ports, some dating from the early 1900s.

Pingo Doce

Rua 1º de Dezembro 123. Most central branch of the supermarket chain – a good place to stock up on picnic fodder, snacks or inexpensive booze. Open daily until 8.30pm.

Cafés

Beira Gare

Rua 1º de Dezembro 5. Daily 6.30am–1am. Well-established café opposite Rossio station, serving stand-up Portuguese snacks and bargain meals. Constantly busy, which is recommendation enough.

Café Garrett

Teatro Nacional de Dona Maria. Tues–Fri 3–4pm & 7.30–10pm, Sat 3–4pm. Lisbon's creative types frequent this theatre café, hidden among the imposing columns of Lisbon's main theatre. Moderately priced cakes, sandwiches and drinks come with views across to the Neo-Manueline Rossio station.

Confeitaria Nacional

Praça da Figueira 18. Daily 8am–8pm, Oct–April closed Sun. Opened in 1829 and little changed since, with a stand-up counter selling pastries and sweets below a mirrored ceiling. There's a little side room and outdoor seating for sit-down coffees and snacks.

Nicola

Rossio 24. Mon–Sat 9am–10pm, Sun 10am–7pm. The only surviving Rossio coffee house from the seventeenth century, once the haunt of some of Lisbon's great literary figures. The outdoor tables overlooking the bustle of Rossio are the café's best feature, though it has sacrificed much of its period interior in the name of modernization. Also has a basement restaurant.

Suíça

Rossio 96. Daily 7am–9pm. Famous for its cakes and pastries; you'll have a hard job getting an outdoor table here, though there's plenty of room inside. The café stretches through to Praça da Figueira, where you'll find the best alfresco seating.

Restaurants

A Berlenga

Rua Barros Queiroz 29. Daily noon–11.30pm. ☎213 422 703. A *cervejaria* restaurant with a window displaying crabs and seafood. Early evening snackers munch prawns at the bar, giving way later on to local diners who tend to eat meals chosen from the window displays, though there are also some meat dishes on the menu. Mains range from €8 to 12.

Adega Santo Antão

Rua das Portas de Santo Antão 42 ☎213 424 188. Tues–Sun noon–midnight. Very good-value and characterful *adega* (wine cellar). There's a bustling bar area, and tables inside and out where you can tuck in to great grilled meat and fish dishes; the sardines are always superb.

Andorra

Rua das Portas de Santo Antão 82 ☎213 426 047. Daily noon–midnight. Boasting an outdoor terrace on one of the broadest stretches of the street, this is the perfect place for people-watching and remains perenially popular with tourists. The Portuguese fish dishes and grills are good but slightly overpriced.

Bom Jardim, Rei dos Frangos

Trav. de Santo Antão 11–18 ☎213 424 389. Daily noon–11.30pm. A bit of a Lisbon institution thanks to its spit-roast chickens and now so popular that it has spread into three buildings on either side of a pedestrianized alley. There are plenty of tables outdoors, too. A half chicken is yours for around €5, though it also serves other meat and fish.

Casa do Alentejo

Rua das Portas de Santo Antão 58 ☎213 469 231. Daily noon–3pm & 7–11pm. As much a centre dedicated to Alentejan culture as a restaurant, "Alentejo House" has an extravagantly decorated interior complete with a stunning inner courtyard and seventeenth-century furniture. Various exhibitions are held here, lending gravitas to the sound Portuguese food served in the two upstairs dining rooms. Mid-priced Alentejo specialities include *sopa à alentejana* (garlic soup with egg) and *carne de porco à alentejana* (grilled pork with clams). Reservations are advised.

▲ RESTAURANT TOUT ON RUA PORTAS DE SANTO ANTÃO

Celeiro

Rua 1° de Dezembro 65 ☎213 422
463. Mon–Fri 8.30am–8pm, Sat
8.30am–7pm. Just off Rossio, this
inexpensive self-service
restaurant in the basement of a
health-food supermarket offers
tasty vegetarian spring rolls,
quiches, pizza and the like from
around €6. Go for the food, not
the decor or ambience.

Gambrinus

Rua das Portas de Santo Antão 15
☎213 421 466. Daily noon–2am.
Rated one of Lisbon's top
seafood restaurants, with a smart,
wood-panelled interior and
crisp, expensive, old-fashioned
service. The menu features
seasonal delights like broiled eel
with bacon, or lobster, and there
are crepes for dessert.
Reservations advised. Mains
from €20–30.

Leão d'Ouro

Rua 1° de Dezembro 105 ☎213 426
195. Daily noon–2pm & 7pm–
midnight. Cool and attractive
azulejo-covered restaurant,
usually frequented more by
tourists than Lisboetas. It
specializes in seafood and
grilled meats and prices are
quite high, but then so is the
quality. Dinner reservations are
advised.

Solar dos Presuntos

Rua das Portas de Santo Antão 150
☎213 424 253. Mon–Sat noon–3pm
& 7–11pm. The "Manor House
of Hams" is, not surprisingly,
best known for its smoked ham
from the Minho region in
northern Portugal, served cold
as a starter. There are also
excellent, if expensive, rice and
game dishes, not to mention a
good wine list; the service can
be overly formal. The daily
specials are good value,
otherwise mains start at
around €15.
Reservations are advised.

Solar

Rua das Portas de Santo
Antão 108 ☎213 423 371.
Daily noon–3pm & 7–10pm.
A cavernous if pricey
seafood restaurant,
complete with fountain
and marine mosaics,
worth a visit as much
for the experience as for
the food, which can be
hit or miss. Splash out
on one of the lobsters in
the bubbling tanks and
you shouldn't leave
disappointed. Despite
the high prices, it's not
above showing live
football on giant TV
screens.

▼ SOLMAR

Bars

A Ginginha

Largo de São Domingos 8. Daily 9am–10.30pm. Everyone should try *ginginha* – Portuguese cherry brandy – once. There's just about room in this microscopic joint to walk in, down a glassful and stagger outside to see the city in a new light.

Ginginha-Rubi

Rua B. Queiroz. Daily 9am–10.30pm. Worth a peer inside for its beautiful azulejos, this tiny watering hole offers *ginginha* with or without the cherry stone (some argue that its presence enhances the alcoholic content).

▲ GINGINHA-RUBI BAR

Hard Rock Café

Avenida da Liberdade 2. Sun–Thurs 11am–2am, Fri & Sat 11am–4am ☏ 213 245 280. Peppered with rock memorabilia and complete with an upside-down car on the roof, the interior is quite a sight. It extends to the full height of the old Condes cinema from which it was hollowed out. Enjoy a drink here, even if the pricey steaks, burgers, cocktails and rock are standard chain fare.

The Sé and around

East of the Baixa, the streets begin to rise steeply up one of Lisbon's many hills. The slopes around the Sé – Lisbon's cathedral – probably helped buffet the area from the worst effects of the 1755 earthquake; though most of the buildings date from the nineteenth century, many are pre-quake survivors.

The Sé

Largo da Sé ☎218 866 752. Daily 9am–7pm. Free. Lisbon's main cathedral, the Sé, was founded in 1150 to commemorate the city's reconquest from the Moors on the site of their main mosque. It's a Romanesque structure with a suitably fortress-like appearance, yet is extraordinarily restrained in both size and decoration. The great rose window and twin towers form a simple and effective facade, although there's nothing particularly exciting inside: the building was once splendidly embellished on the orders of Dom João V, but his Rococo whims were swept away by the 1755 earthquake and subsequent restorers. All that remains is a group of Gothic tombs behind the high altar and the decaying thirteenth-century **cloister** (Mon–Sat 10am–6pm, Sun 2–6pm; €2.50). This is currently being heavily excavated, revealing the remains of a sixth-century Roman house and Moorish public buildings.

The Baroque **Treasury** (Mon–Sat 10am–5pm; €2.50) holds a small museum of treasures including the relics of Saint Vincent, brought to Lisbon in 1173 in a boat that was piloted by ravens, according to legend. Ravens were kept in the cloisters for centuries afterwards, but the tradition halted when the last one died in 1978. To this day, however, the birds remain one of the city's symbols.

▼ THE SÉ

Igreja de Santo António and Museu Antoniano

Largo S. António da Sé ☎218 869 145. The eighteenth-century church of **Santo**

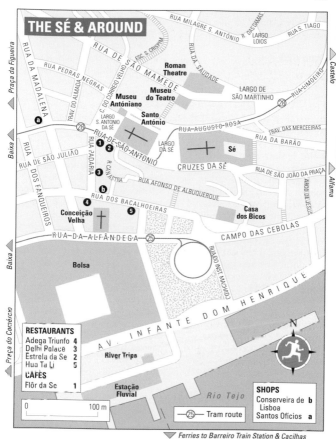

The map shows:

THE SÉ & AROUND

RUA MILAGRE S. ANTÓNIO · R. DAS DAMAS · RUA S. TIAGO · LARGO LOIOS

Castelo

RUA DE SÃO MAMEDE · ESC. S. CRISPIM · RUA DA SAUDADE

RUA DA ALMADA · TRAV. DO ALMADA · RUA PEDRAS NEGRAS · C. C. DO CORREIO VELHO

Praça da Figueira

RUA DA MADALENA

Roman Theatre

Museu Antóniano · Museu do Teatro

LARGO DE SÃO MARTINHO

RUA-LIMOEIRO

Baixa

LARGO S. ANTONIO DA SÉ

Santo António

RUA-DE-SÃO-ANTÓNIO

RUA DE SÃO JULIÃO

RUA PADARIA

LARGO DA SÉ

RUA-AUGUSTO-ROSA

RUA DA BARÃO

TRAV. DAS MERCEEIRAS

Sé

Alfama

RUA DOS FANQUEIROS

R. CANASTRA

CRUZES DA SÉ

RUA DE SÃO JOÃO DA PRAÇA

RUA AFONSO DE ALBUQUERQUE

ARCO DE JESUS

Conceição Velha

RUA DOS BACALHOEIROS

Casa dos Bicos

Baixa

RUA-DA-ALFÂNDEGA

CAMPO DAS CEBOLAS

Bolsa

RUA DO INST. MACHADO

Praça do Comércio

A. V. INFANTE DOM HENRIQUE

River Trips

RESTAURANTS
Adega Triunfo 4
Delhi Palace 3
Estrela da Sé 2
Hua Ta Li 5

CAFÉS
Flôr da Sé 1

Estação Fluvial

Rio Tejo

N

0   100 m

25 — Tram route

SHOPS
Conserveira de **b**
Lisboa
Santos Ofícios **a**

▽ Ferries to Barreiro Train Station & Cacilhas

António (open daily) is said to
have been built on the spot
where the city's most popular
saint was born as Fernando
Bulhões; after his death in Italy
he became known as Saint
Anthony of Padua. The tiny
neighbouring **museum**
(Tues–Sat 10am–1pm & 2–
6pm, Sun 10am–1pm; €1.20,
free Sun) chronicles the saint's
life, including his enviable skill
at fixing marriages, though
only devotees will find interest
in the statues and endless
images.

Conceição Velha

Rua da Alfandega ☎218 870 202.
Mon–Sat 8am–6pm, Sun 10am–1pm.
Free. The church of Conceição
Velha was severely damaged by
the 1755 earthquake, but is still
in possession of its flamboyant
fifteenth-century Manueline
doorway. This is an early
example of the brilliant
architectural style named after
the reign of Dom Manuel, king
of Portugal, during the great
age of discoveries. The interior
of the church, however, rebuilt
after the earthquake, is

relatively plain, with just one nave.

Tram #25

The open area to the east of Conceição Velha is the terminus for another of Lisbon's classic tram rides, the #25, which sees far fewer tourists than tram #28 but takes almost as picturesque a route. From here it trundles along the riverfront and up through Lapa and Estrela to the suburb of Prazeres, best known as the site of one of Lisbon's largest cemeteries. You can stroll round the enormous plot where family tombs are movingly adorned with trinkets and photos of the deceased.

Casa dos Bicos

Rua dos Bacalhoeiros ☎ 218 810 900. Mon–Fri 9.30am–5.30pm. Free. The Casa dos Bicos means the "House of Points", and its curious walls – set with diamond-shaped stones – give an idea of the richness of pre-1755 Lisbon. It was built in 1523 for the son of the Viceroy of India, though only the facade of the original building survived the earthquake. It is in fairly regular use as the venue for cultural exhibitions; at other times, you can look around the remains of Roman fish-preserving tanks and parts of Lisbon's old Moorish walls (demolished in the fifteenth century).

Museu do Teatro Romano

Entrance on Patio de Aljube 5 ☎ 218 885 958; ⊛ www.museu-teatroromano .net. Tues–Sun 10am–1pm & 2–6pm. Free. The Museu do Teatro Romano displays Roman coins, spoons and fragments of pots, statues and columns excavated from the sparse ruins of a Roman theatre, dating from 57 AD, which are fenced off just north of Rua Augusto Rosa. Roman Lisbon – Olisipo – became the administrative capital of Lusitania, the western part of Iberia, under Julius Caesar in 60 BC, and the theatre shows the wealth that quickly grew thanks to its fish-preserving industries.

▼ TINNED FISH IN CONSERVEIRA DE LISBOA

Shops

Conserveira de Lisboa
Rua dos Bacalhoeiras 34. Wall-to-wall tin cans stuffed into wooden cabinets make this colourful 1930s' shop a bizarre but intriguing place to stock up on tinned sardines, squid, salmon, mussels and just about any other sea beast you can think of.

Santos Ofícios
Rua da Madalena 87. Small shop crammed with a somewhat touristy collection of regional crafts, but including some attractive ceramics, rugs, embroidery, baskets and toys.

Cafés

Flôr da Sé
Largo da Sé. Mon–Sat 7am–8pm. Convenient *pastelaria* with a counter packed with pastries and savouries. Tables are set out beneath azulejos depicting Santo António. It also does decent, inexpensive lunches.

Restaurants

Adega Triunfo
Rua dos Bacalhoeiros 129 ☎218 869 840. Tues–Sun noon–midnight. One of the best of the moderately priced café-restaurants along this street. It has a changing menu of meat and fish dishes, pricier seafood and cheap house wine. The *feijoada* (bean stew) is a good bet, and the air-conditioning comes into its own in high summer.

Delhi Palace
Rua da Padaria 18–20 ☎218 884 203. Mon–Sat noon–3.30pm & 6pm–midnight. Offers decent curries for a good price. The Goan prawn curry is excellent, and there is a good range of vegetarian and tandoori dishes. Friendly, English-speaking Indian owners.

Estrela da Sé
Largo S. António da Sé 4 ☎218 870 455. Mon–Fri noon–3pm & 7–11pm. Beautiful azulejo-covered restaurant near the Sé, serving inexpensive and tasty dishes like *alheira* (chicken sausage), salmon and Spanish-style tapas. Its wooden booths – perfect for discreet trysts – date from the nineteenth century.

Hua Ta Li
Rua dos Bacalhoeiros 119 ☎218 879 170. Daily noon–3.30pm & 6.30–11pm. Very good value Chinese restaurant, especially popular for Sunday lunch, when it heaves with people (so it's best to book). Seafood scores highly; try the squid chop suey. It's also good for vegetarians.

The Alfama and the riverfront

The oldest and most atmospheric part of Lisbon, Alfama was buttressed against significant damage in the 1755 earthquake by the steep, rocky mass on which it's built. Although none of its houses dates from before the Christian Reconquest, many are of Moorish design with a kasbah-like layout.

In Moorish times this was the grandest part of the city, but as Lisbon expanded, the new Christian nobility moved out, leaving it to the local fishing community. Today, although tourist shops and fado restaurants are moving in, the quarter retains a quiet, village-like quality. Life continues much as it has done for years in the labyrinthine streets, with people buying groceries and fish from hole-in-the-wall stores and householders stringing washing across narrow defiles and stoking small outdoor charcoal grills. Half the fun of exploring here is getting lost but, at some point, head for Rua de São Miguel – off which run some of the most interesting *becos* (alleys) – and for the parallel street Rua de São Pedro, where *varinas* (fishwives) sell the catch of the day from tiny stalls.

Casa do Fado e da Guitarra Portuguesa

Largo do Chafariz de Dentro ☎218 823 470. Daily 10am–1pm & 2–6pm. €2.50. Set in the renovated Recinto da Praia, a former water cistern and bathhouse, the Casa do Fado e da Guitarra Portuguesa provides an excellent introduction to fado, the mournful Portuguese musical sound that emerged from the Alfama alleys. The museum details the history of fado and

Fado

Fado (literally "fate") is often described as a kind of Portuguese blues. Popular themes are love, death, destiny, bullfighting and indeed fate itself. It is believed to derive from music that was popular with eighteenth-century immigrants from Portugal's colonies who first settled in Alfama. Famous singers like Maria Severa and Amália Rodrigues grew up in Alfama, which since the 1930s has hosted some of the city's most authentic fado houses. The big contemporary name is Mariza, who grew up in neighbouring Mouraria. Other singers to look out for (though unlikely to appear in small venues) are Mizia, Helder Moutinho, Carlos do Carmo, Maria da Fe and Cristina Branco, though you may find the most entertaining fado of all is performed spontaneously by amateurs in bars and restaurants.

its importance to the Portuguese people; its shop stocks a great selection of CDs. A series of rooms in the museum containing wax models, pictures and descriptions of fado's leading characters also trace the history of the Portuguese guitar, an essential element of the fado performance. You can push buttons to listen to the different types of fado (Lisbon has its own kind, differing from that of the northern city of Coimbra), varying from mournful to positively racy.

Doca do Jardim do Tobaco

On the riverfront, across the busy Avenida Infante Dom Henrique, lies the dockland development of the Doca do Jardim do Tobaco. Its name, "Tobacco Garden Dock", refers to its previous role as the city's main depot for storing tobacco. The old warehouses, facing one of the broadest sections of the Rio Tejo, have been spruced up and it's a great place for a sunset drink or an evening meal with the views from the outdoor tables of its restaurants attracting a largely local crowd.

Miradouro de Santa Luzia

The church of Santa Luzia marks the entry to the Miradouro de Santa Luzia, a spectacular viewpoint where elderly Lisboetas play cards and tourists gather to take in the sweeping views across the Alfama and the river beyond. Opposite is the main, well-signposted route up to the entrance to the Castelo de São Jorge (see p.74).

Museu de Artes Decorativas

Museum Largo das Portas do Sol 2 ☎218 881 991, Ⓦwww.fress.pt. Mon–Sat 10am–5pm. €5. Set in the

▲ ALFAMA STREET

seventeenth-century Azurara Palace, this fascinating museum contains some of the best examples of sixteenth- to eighteenth-century applied art in the country. Founded by a wealthy banker and donated to the nation in 1953, the museum boasts unique pieces of furniture, major collections of gold, silver and porcelain, magnificent paintings and textiles. The rambling building covers five floors, set around a stairway decorated with spectacular azulejos. Highlights include a stunning sixteenth-century tapestry depicting a parade of giraffes, beautiful carpets from Arraiolos in the Alentejo district, and oriental-influenced quilts that were all the rage during the seventeenth and eighteenth centuries. The museum also has a small if expensive café with a patio garden.

Cafés

Miradouro de Santa Luzia

Miradouro de Santa Luzia. Daily 10am–10pm. Hilltop suntrap just below the viewpoint of the

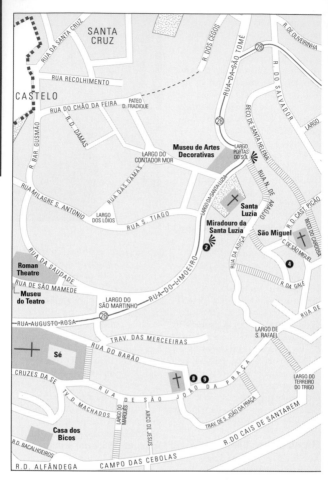

same name. Drinks and meals are slightly pricey but you pay for the views, which are fabulous.

Pois Café
Rua São João da Praça 93–95. Tues–Sun 11am–8pm. With its big comfy sofas and laid-back ambience, walking into this Austrian-run café here feels like going into someone's large front room. There's a friendly, young crowd, light meals and home-made snacks, including a great *apfelstrudel*. Recommended.

Restaurants

Jardim do Mariscos
Avda Infante Dom Henrique, Doca do Jardim do Tobaco Pavilhão A/B ☎218 824 240. Daily 1pm–midnight. Best-positioned in the row of pricey warehouse restaurants in the Doca Jardim do Tobaco

THE ALFAMA & THE RIVERFRONT

CALC. DO TIJOLO
C. DE SÃO VICENTE
RUA-DES-ESCOLAS-GERAIS
RUA DAS ESCOLAS
DO SALVADOR RUA G BRAGA
RUA DOS CORVOS
ALFAMA
RUA DES VIGÁRIO
LARGO DO PENEIREIRO
Santo Estêvão
RUA SANTO ESTEVÃO
RUA DA B. DO CARNEIRO
RUA DOS REMEDIOS
BECO DA LAPA
LARGO DO CHAFARIZ DE DENTRO
RUA DE SÃO MIGUEL
BECO D. AZINHAL
RUA D. JARDIM DO TABACO
Casa do Fado
REGUEIRA
PÓCINHO
SÃO PEDRO
BECO DOS LORTIMES
RUA TERREIRO DO TRIGO
CAS DA LINGUETA
AVENIDA INFANTE DOM HENRIQUE
Doca do Jardim do Tobaco
Doca do Terreiro do Trigo

N

❶ ❸ ❺ ❻ ❼ ❿

─25─ Tram route

0 .... 100 m

PLACES

The Alfama and the riverfront

development, the counter by the main entrance groans under the weight of crabs, giant prawns and shellfish and, not surprisingly, seafood is the speciality – grilled, served in salads, or with pasta or *açorda* (a garlic and bread sauce). There's an upstairs terrace with great river views and an airy interior with high ceilings.

Lautasco
Beco do Azinhal 7 ☏ 218 860 173.
Mon–Sat 10am–3pm & 9–11.30pm;

▼ MIRADOURO DE SANTA LUZIA

closed Dec. Tucked just off the Largo do Chafariz de Dentro, in a picturesque Alfama courtyard; by day a shady retreat, by night a magical, fairy-lit oasis. Multilingual menus and higher than usual prices suggest a largely tourist clientele but it's a great spot for *borrego* (lamb), *tamboril* (monkfish) or *cataplanas* (stews). Bookings are advised. Mains from around €15.

Malmequer-Bemmequer

Rua de São Miguel 23–25 ☎ 218 876 535. Wed–Sun 12.30–3.30pm & 7–10.30pm, Tues 7–10.30pm; closed last week in Oct. Cheerily decorated and moderately priced place, overseen by a friendly owner. Grilled meat and fish dishes dominate the menu (try the *salmão no carvão* – charcoal-grilled salmon), or eat from the daily changing tourist menu for around €15.

▼ NARROW ALLEY DINING IN ALFAMA

Maria da Fonte

Rua de São Pedro 5a ☎ 218 876 896. Tues–Sun noon–2am. Tiny, intimate tiled restaurant with good-value fish dishes. The speciality is *bife na pedra* (steak cooked on a hot stone). Come here from Thursday to Sunday and you'll be treated to live fado from 8pm.

Santo António de Alfama

Beco de São Miguel 7 ☎ 218 881 328 or 218 881 329. Daily except Tues 8pm–2am. With black-and-white photos of film stars on the wall and a lovely outdoor terrace shaded by vines, this is one of the nicest restaurant-bars in the Alfama; it's off Rua de São Miguel, and you should book to guarantee a table. There's a very long list of expensive wines, but the food (dishes like *carpaccio de salmão* – salmon carpaccio – and game sausages) is more moderately priced.

Live music

Clube do Fado

Rua de São João da Praça 92–94 ☎ 218 852 704. Daily 8.30pm–2am. Intimate and homely fado club with stone pillars, an old well as a decorative feature, and a mainly local clientele. It attracts small-time performers, up-and-coming talent and the occasional big name. Minimum charge is around €15, though add in food and it will be nearer €40.

▲ IGREJA DE SÃO MIGUEL, ALFAMA

noon–2am. Dockside bar with fine river views and live music most nights from 11.30pm, usually from Thursday to Sunday. Sounds range from flamenco and folk to occasional rock.

A Parreirinha de Alfama

Beco do Espírito Santo 1 ☎ 218 868 209. Daily 8pm–2am. One of the best fado venues, just off Largo do Chafariz de Dentro, often attracting leading stars and an enthusiastic local clientele. Reservations are advised when the big names appear. The minimum charge is around €15, but expect to spend about €30 with food.

Musicais

Doca do Jardim do Tabaco Pavilhao A/B ⓦ www.musicaio.com. Daily

Castelo, Mouraria and Graça

The remains of the Castelo de São Jorge form a little oasis of tranquillity in a fantastic position high above the city. The castle and the surrounding ancient districts of Mouraria and Santa Cruz are, along with Alfama, the oldest and most interesting areas of Lisbon. To get an aerial view of this neighbourhood, head to the nearby district of Graça, which sits next to Lisbon's highest hill.

Castelo de São Jorge

☎218 800 2620. Daily: March–Oct 9am–9pm; Nov–Feb 9am–6pm. €3 includes visit to Câmara Escura and Olisipónia. Bus #37 from Praça da Figueira. Reached by a confusing but well-signposted series of twisting roads, the Castelo de São Jorge is perhaps the most spectacular building in Lisbon, as much because of its position as anything else. Justly Lisbon's most-visited tourist site, the

▼ VIEW FROM CASTLE

castle's current function is far removed from its historical role. This was once the heart of a walled city that spread downhill as far as the river. The castle's fortifications were strengthened after the original Moorish castle was besieged in 1147 by a particularly ruthless gang of Crusaders who conquered Lisbon after some four hundred years of Moorish rule. From the fourteenth century, Portuguese kings took up residence in the old Moorish palace, or Alcáçova, within the walls, but by the early sixteenth century they had moved to the new royal palace on Praça do Comércio. Subsequently, the castle was used as a prison for a time and then as an army barracks until the 1920s. The walls were partly renovated by Salazar in the 1930s and further restored for the Expo 98. A series of gardens, walkways and viewpoints hidden within the old Moorish walls makes this an enjoyable place in which to wander about for a couple of hours, with spectacular views over the city from its ramparts and towers.

Câmara Escura

March–Oct, weather permitting, at 10am, 1pm, 2pm & 5.30 pm; closed

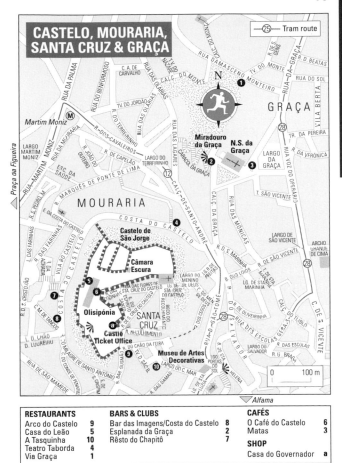

CASTELO, MOURARIA, SANTA CRUZ & GRAÇA

―25― Tram route

RESTAURANTS		BARS & CLUBS		CAFÉS	
Arco do Castelo	9	Bar das Imagens/Costa do Castelo	8	O Café do Castelo	6
Casa do Leão	5	Esplanada da Graça	2	Matas	3
A Tasquinha	10	Rêsto do Chapitô	7		
Teatro Taborda	4			**SHOP**	
Via Graça	1			Casa do Governador	a

Jan 1, May 1 & Dec 25. One of the castle towers, the Tower of Ulysses, now holds a kind of periscope which projects sights from around the city onto a white disk with commentary in English. Unless you like being holed up in dark chambers with up to fifteen other people, though, you may prefer to see the view in the open air.

The Alcáçova and Olisipónia
Daily: May–Sept 10am–1pm & 2–6pm; Oct–April 10am–1pm & 2–5.30pm. Of

the old Moorish Alcáçova, only a much-restored shell remains. This now houses Olisipónia (the Roman name for the city), a multimedia history shown in three underground chambers. Portable headsets provide a 35-minute commentary on aspects of Lisbon's development; although the presentations overlap somewhat and gloss over a few of Lisbon's less savoury chapters, such as slavery and the Inquisition, they are a useful introduction to the city.

Santa Cruz and Mouraria

Crammed within the castle's outer walls is the tiny medieval quarter of Santa Cruz. Despite the opening of the exclusive *Solar do Castelo* hotel (see p.171), this remains a village in its own right, with its own school, bathhouse and church. Wander round and you'll find kids playing in the streets and housewives chatting on doorsteps – and little else. Leaving Santa Cruz, a tiny arch at the end of Rua do Chão da Feira leads through to Rua dos Cegos and down to Largo Rodrigues de Freitas, which marks the eastern edge of Mouraria, the district to which the Moors were relegated after the siege of Lisbon – hence the name. Today Mouraria is an atmospheric residential area with some of the city's best African restaurants, especially around Largo de São Cristóvão.

Graça

The ever-popular tram #28 (see next) passes the broad Largo da Graça on its way to its final stop in Largo Martim Moniz. Head past Nossa Senhora da Graça – a church which partly dates from 1271 – to Miradouro da Graça, where you can admire superb views over Lisbon and the castle.

Tram #28

The picture-book tram #28 is one of the city's greatest rides, though its popularity is such that there are usually queues to get on and standing-room only is more than likely. Built in England in the early twentieth century, the trams are all polished wood and chrome but give a distinctly rough ride up and down Lisbon's steepest streets, at times coming so close to shops that you could almost take a can of sardines off the shelves. From Graça, the tram plunges down through Alfama to the Baixa and up to Prazeres, to the west of the centre.

Shops

Casa do Governador

Castelo de São Jorge. Daily 10am–1pm & 2–6pm. Right by the castle entrance, the former Governor of Lisbon's house is now a shop with a somewhat sparse and eclectic collection of art books, black-and-white postcards of old Lisbon, fado and world music CDs, and some tasteful ceramics.

▼ O CAFÉ DO CASTELO

Cafés

O Café do Castelo

Castelo de São Jorge. Daily 9am–
dusk. Set within the castle walls,
this café offers good-value
buffet lunches (all you can eat
for €8) and drinks. Its outdoor
tables are beautifully positioned
under shady trees, with the
castle's resident peacocks for
company.

Matas

Largo da Graça 63C/D. Mon–Sat
8am–8pm. Handily across the
square from the tram #28 stop,
this little café in a completely
tiled building has tables inside
or out for drinks and
inexpensive lunches such as
salads and grills.

Restaurants

Arco do Castelo

Rua do Chão da Feira 25 ☏ 218 876
598. Mon–Sat noon–midnight.
Cheerful place just below the
entrance to the castle,
specializing in moderately
priced Goan dishes – choose
from tempting shrimp curry,
Indian sausage or spicy seafood.
Mains are from €8.

Casa do Leão

Castelo de São Jorge ☏ 218 875 962.
Daily 12.30–3pm & 8–11pm. Owned
by the Pousada hotel group, this
restaurant within the city walls
couldn't be better situated,
providing a superb city view
from its outside terrace and tiled
interior. Service is slick and the
top-rate traditional Portuguese
food includes *cataplana de cherne*
(seabass) or lobster. Mains
around €20 though seafood
hikes up the bill. Reservations
are advised.

A Tasquinha

Largo do Contador Mor 5–7. Mon–Sat
10am–11pm. Considering its
position on the main route up
to the castle, this lovely *tasca*
(dining room) has remained
remarkably unaffected by
tourism. The food – grilled fish
and chicken – is good value, too,
served either at the few tables in
the traditionally decorated
interior, or on the fine outdoor
terrace.

Teatro Taborda

Costa do Castelo 75 ☏ 218 879 484.
Tues–Sun 2pm–midnight.
Fashionable theatre café-
restaurant with fine views from
the terrace. The menu offers
inexpensive fish and fresh
vegetarian dishes, including
vegetable lasagne, Greek salad
and falafels from €4.

Via Graça

Rua Damasceno Monteiro 9b ☏ 218
870 830. Mon–Fri 12.30–3.30pm &
7.30pm–midnight, Sat 7.30pm–
midnight. Tucked away below the
Miradouro da Graça (take a left
after Largo da Graça becomes
Rua da Graça), this smart and
expensive restaurant in an
unattractive modern building is
a whole lot better on the inside,
from where you can soak up the
stunning panoramas of Lisbon.
Specialities include partridge
with clam *cataplana* and lobster
and *bacalhau* with spider crab.

Bars and clubs

Bar das Imagens/Costa do Castelo

Calçada do Marquês de Tancos 1b
☏ 218 884 636. March–Dec Wed–Sat
4pm–2am, Sun 3pm–9pm. Beautifully
positioned terrace-café with
Baixa views, a long list of
cocktails and a restaurant serving

▲ TERRACE OF CASA DO LEÃO

Graça. It's not cheap, but the seats have stunning views over the bridge and the Baixa, particularly at sunset. After dark, it cranks up a powerful music system to change the atmosphere from laid-back to decidedly lively.

Rêsto do Chapitô

Costa do Castelo 1–7 ☎218 867 334. ⊛www.chapito.org. Restaurant Tues–Fri 7.30pm–2am, Sat & Sun noon–2am. Bar daily 9pm–2pm. Multipurpose venue incorporating a theatre, circus school, restaurant and jazz bar. The restaurant is in an upstairs dining room, reached via a spiral staircase, and serves moderately priced pastas, salads and one or two fish and meat dishes. The outdoor esplanade commands terrific views over Alfama and most people come here to drink and take in the view. The jazz bar offers live music most weekend evenings (call for info on ☎218 880 406) and films, readings and Internet access at other times.

mid-price salads and pasta dishes. There's live music (usually Brazilian or jazz) on Thursday and Friday nights, and occasional poetry readings at other times.

Esplanada da Graça

Largo da Graça ☎217 427 508. Daily, weather permitting, 10am–2am. A tiny kiosk serving coffee, drinks and snacks by the Miradouro da

Eastern Lisbon

East of the castle on the periphery of the Alfama lie two of Lisbon's most historic and prominent churches, São Vicente de Fora and Santa Engrácia. These both deserve a visit, as does the twice-weekly rambling Feira da Ladra flea market that enlivens the area. Down on the riverfront, Santa Apolónia, Lisbon's main international train station, is situated in a revitalized area that boasts the city's most fashionable club, Lux. The industrial dock area east of here is of less interest, apart from the fascinating tile museum, a short bus ride away.

São Vicente de Fora

Tues–Sat 9am–6pm, Sat 9am–7pm, Sun 9am–12.30pm & 3–5pm. Free.
The church of São Vicente de Fora stands as a reminder of the extent of the sixteenth-century city; its name means "Saint Vincent of the Outside". It was built during the years of Spanish rule by Philip II's Italian architect, Felipe Terzi (1582–1629); its severe geometric facade was an important Renaissance innovation. Through the cloisters, decorated with azulejos representing scenes from Portugal's history, you can visit the old monastic refectory, which since 1855 has formed the **pantheon of the Bragança dynasty** (Tues–Sun 10am–6pm; €4). Here, in more or less complete sequence, are the tombs of all the Portuguese kings from João IV, who restored the monarchy in 1640, to Manuel II, the last Portuguese monarch who died in exile in England in 1932. Among them is Catherine of Bragança, the widow of England's Charles II, who is credited as having introduced the concept of "teatime" to the Brits. There's a café (see p.81) at the church if you do fancy a cup of tea.

Feira da Ladra

Tues and Sat 9am–around 3pm.
The broad, leafy square of Campo de Santa Clara is home to the twice-weekly Feira da Ladra ("Thieves' Market"), Lisbon's main flea market. It's not the world's greatest market, but it does turn up some interesting things, like oddities from the former African colonies and old

▲ SÃO VICENTE DE FORA

PLACES

Eastern Lisbon

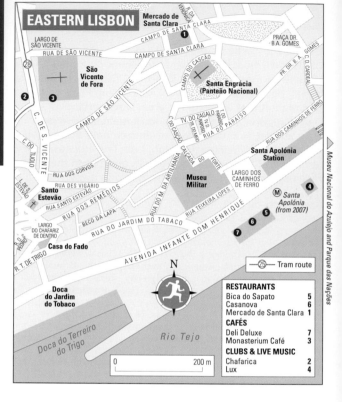

EASTERN LISBON

Mercado de Santa Clara ❶

LARGO DE SÃO VICENTE

RUA DE SÃO VICENTE

CAMPO DE SANTA CLARA

CAMPO DE SANTA CLARA

PRAÇA DR. B.A. GOMES

São Vicente de Fora

❷ ❸

C. DE S. VICENTE

CAMPO DO CAÇÃO

Santa Engrácia (Panteão Nacional)

CAMPO DE SÃO VICENTE

C. DO TIJOLO

RUA DOS CORVOS

RUA DES VIGÁRIO

Santo Estevão

RUA SANTO ESTEVÃO

RUA DOS REMÉDIOS

BECO DA LAPA

Museu Militar

Santa Apolónia Station

LARGO DOS CAMINHOS DE FERRO

Ⓜ Santa Apolónia (from 2007)

❹

RUA TEIXEIRA LOPES

❻ ❺

❼

LARGO DO CHAFARIZ DE DENTRO

RUA DO JARDIM DO TABACO

Casa do Fado

AVENIDA INFANTE DOM HENRIQUE

N

Doca do Jardim do Tobaco

Doca do Terreiro do Trigo

Rio Tejo

—Ⓣ25— Tram route

0   200 m

RESTAURANTS
Bica do Sapato   5
Casanova   6
Mercado de Santa Clara   1
CAFÉS
Deli Deluxe   7
Monasterium Café   3
CLUBS & LIVE MUSIC
Chafarica   2
Lux   4

Museu Nacional do Azulejo and Parque das Nações

Portuguese prints. Out-and-out junk – from broken alarm clocks to old postcards – is spread on the ground above Santa Engrácia, with cheap clothes, CDs and half-genuine antiques at the top end of the *feira*. The covered *mercado* (market) building has a fine array of fresh fruit and vegetables.

Santa Engrácia

Tues–Sun: May–Oct 10am–6pm; Nov–April 10am–5pm. €2, free Sun 10am–2pm. The white dome of Santa Engrácia makes it one of the most recognizable buildings on the city skyline. The loftiest church in the city, it has become synonymous with unfinished

work – begun in 1682, it was only completed in 1966. It is now the **Panteão Nacional**, housing the tombs of eminent Portuguese figures, including writer Almeida Garrett (1799–1854) and Amália Rodrigues (1920–1999), Portugal's most famous fado singer. You can take the stairs up to the terrace, from where there are great views over the flea market, port and city.

Museu Nacional do Azulejo

Rua da Madre de Deus 4 ☎218 103 340. Tues 2–6pm, Wed–Sun 10am–6pm. €3, free Sun 10am–2pm. Bus #104 or bus #105 from Praça do Comércio/Santa Apolonia. The Museu Nacional do Azulejo (tile museum) traces the development of the distinctive Portuguese azulejo tiles from fifteenth-century Moorish styles to the present day, with each room representing a different style and period. Styles are wonderfully diverse: look out for the seventeenth-century portraits of Britain's King Charles II with his Portuguese wife, Catherine of Bragança, the stunning seventeenth-century decorative Goan tiles and a 1720 satirical panel depicting a man being given an injection in his bottom. The museum is inside the church **Madre de Deus**, whose eighteenth-century-tiled scenes of the life of St Anthony are among the best in the city. Many of the rooms are housed round the church's cloisters – look for the spire in one corner of the main cloister, itself completely tiled. Upstairs there are some of the best contemporary tiles. The highlight here is Portugal's longest azulejo – a wonderfully detailed forty-metre panorama of Lisbon, completed in around 1738. The museum café-restaurant is a great spot for lunch, with meals taken in the leafy garden and there's also a good shop selling high-quality azulejos.

Cafés

Deli Deluxe

Avda Infante Dom Henrique, Armazem B, Loja 8. Tues–Fri noon–10pm, Sat 10am–10pm, Sun 10am–8pm. A modern deli with delectable cheeses, cured meats and preserves, though the riverside café at the back is even more appealing. Grab a seat outdoors and enjoy the range of goodies from croissants to speciality teas, yoghurts, bagels, salads and cocktails. At weekend the set brunches, from €8, are superb.

Monasterium Café

Igreja São Vincente de Fora, Calçada de São Vicente ☏ 218 885 652. Tues–Sun 10am–5pm. The São Vicente monastery café boasts comfortable indoor seating, a tranquil patio and, best of all, a small roof terrace with stupendous views over Alfama and the Tejo (including an aerial view of tram #28 squeezing through its narrowest street).

Restaurants

Bica do Sapato

Avda Infante Dom Henrique, Armazém B, Cais da Pedra à Bica do Sapato ☏

PLACES Eastern Lisbon

▼ VIEW OVER EASTERN LISBON AND SANTA ENGRÁCIA

▼ VIEW OVER EASTERN LISBON AND SANTA ENGRÁCIA

218 810 320. Mon 5pm–2am, Tues–Sat 9am–2am. Part-owned by actor John Malkovich, this very stylish but refreshingly informal warehouse conversion has mirrored walls to reflect the crisp Tejo vistas. There's an outside terrace, too. The chef creates what he calls a "laboratory of Portuguese ingredients", including hare with rice and a fabulous "crustacean mix" of crabs and tiger prawns. Satisfied guests have included Pedro Almodóvar, Catherine Denueve and architect Frank Gehry, though its prices are affordable to mere mortals. Reservations are advised.

Casanova

Avda Infante Dom Henrique, Loja 7 Armazém B, Cais da Pedra à Bica do Sapato ☎218 877 532. Tues 6pm–1.30am, Wed–Sun 12.30pm–1.30am. If *Bica do Sapato* is beyond your budget, the more modestly priced *Casanova* next door offers pizza, pasta and *crostini* accompanied by similar views from its outside terrace. It's phenomenally popular and you can't book, so turn up early.

Mercado de Santa Clara

Campo de Santa Clara ☎218 873 986.

▼ THE MARKET, MERCADO DE SANTA CLARA

Tues–Sat 12.30–3pm & 8pm–midnight, Sun 12.30–3pm. Top-notch cuisine is served in the upstairs room of the old market building, with distant views of the Tejo. Come on Tuesday or Saturday lunchtime to be in the thick of the Feira da Ladra market bustle. The restaurant specializes in moderately priced beef dishes, but also serves more expensive fish, while on Sunday *feijoada* is the dish of the day. Reservations are advised.

Clubs and live music

Chafarica

Calçada de São Vicente 79 ☎218 867 449. Mon–Sat 9pm–3.30am. Long-established Brazilian club with live music every night from around 11pm. It's best after midnight, especially after a few *caipirinhas*, the lethal Brazilian concoction of rum, lime, sugar and ice.

Lux

Armazéns A, Cais da Pedra a Santa Apolónia, ⊛www.lux@luxfragil.com. Tues–Fri 6pm–6am, Sat & Sun 4pm–6am. This converted former meat warehouse has become one of Europe's most fashionable spaces, attracting visiting stars like Prince and Cameron Diaz. Part-owned by actor John Malkovich, it was the first place to venture into the docks opposite Santa Apolónia station. There's a rooftop terrace with amazing views, various bars, projection screens, a frenzied downstairs dance floor, and music from pop and trance to jazz and dance. The club is also increasingly on the circuit for touring bands.

Cais do Sodré and Chiado

The area west of the Baixa presents two very different faces of Lisbon. Down on the waterfront, Cais do Sodré (pronounced kaiysh doo soodray) is a characterful, slightly down-at-heel suburb enlivened by some good restaurants, clubs and bars. Many of its waterfront warehouses have been converted into upmarket cafés and restaurants and by day, in particular, a stroll along its atmospheric riverfront is very enjoyable. Nearby Mercado da Ribeira, Lisbon's main market, is also big on atmosphere, as is the hillside Bica district, which is served by another of the city's classic funicular street lifts – Elevador da Bica. Rising above Cais do Sodré both literally and metaphorically, the well-to-do district of Chiado (pronounced she-ar-doo) is famed for its smart shops and cafés, along with the city's main museum for contemporary arts. It was greatly damaged by a fire in 1988, although the original Belle Époque atmosphere has since been superbly recreated under the direction of eminent Portuguese architect Álvaro Siza Vieira.

Mercado da Ribeira

ⓦwww.espacoribeira.pt The Mercado da Ribeira is Lisbon's main and most interesting market. Built originally on the site of an old fort at the end of the nineteenth century, the current structure dates only from 1930. The main market downstairs (Mon–Sat 6am–2pm) has an impressive array of food and fish of all shapes and sizes – there are also spices, fruit and vegetables. In the past it was traditional for Lisboetas to enjoy a *cacau da Ribeira* (cocoa) here after a night out on the town, and the local council recently decided to renovate the market building in an attempt to restore this social function. As a result, the upper level now boasts a shop and bustling restaurant (see p.88). At weekends, live music ranging from jazz to folk is

▼ FISH AT THE MERCADO DA RIBEIRA

△ Bairro Alto

CAIS DO SODRÉ & CHIADO

RESTAURANTS		BARS & CLUBS		CAFÉS		SHOPS	
Associação Católica	14	Bicaense	8	Bernard	4	Ana Salazar	a
O Canteiro	13	British Bar	15	A Brasileira	6	Armazéns do Chiado	d
Chez Degroote	12	Heróis	3	Café No Chiado	10	Fábrica Sant'anna	f
Comida da Ribeira	17	Hotel Bairro Alto	7	Café Vertigo	1	José Dias Sobral	g
L'Entrecôte	9	The Pump House	11	Wagons-Lit	18	Livraria Bertrand	e
Porto de Abrigo	16	Vou ão Camões	5			Loja de Artesanato	h
Tavares Rico	2					Luvaria Ulisses	b
						Torres and Brinkmann	c

performed either on a central
stage or in the pub-like
RibeirArte Café in the south-
west corner of the upper level.

Elevador da Bica

Mon–Sat 7am–9pm, Sun 9am–9pm.
€1.20. With its entrance tucked
into an arch on Rua de São
Paulo, the Elevador da Bica is
one of the city's most
atmospheric funicular railways.
Built in 1892 – and originally
powered by water
counterweights, but now
electrically operated – the
elevador leads up towards the
Bairro Alto, via a steep
residential street with drying

laundry usually draped from
every window. Take time to
explore the steep side streets of
the Bica neighbourhood, too, a
warren of characterful houses
and little shops.

Miradouro de Santa Catarina

Set on the edge of a cusp of hill
high above the river, the railed
Miradouro de Santa Catarina
has spectacular views. Here, in
the shadow of the statue of the
Adamastor – a mythical beast
from Luís de Camões's *Lusiads* –
a mixture of oddballs and
guitar-strumming New Age
hippies often collects around the
drinks kiosk (daily 10am–dusk,

weather permitting), which has a few outdoor tables.

Museu do Chiado

Rua Serpa Pinto 4 ☎ 213 432 148 ⓦ www.museudochiado-ipmuseus.pt. Tues–Sun 10am–6pm. €3, free Sun 10am–2pm. The Museu do Chiado, Lisbon's contemporary art museum, is a stylish building with a pleasant courtyard café and rooftop terrace, constructed around a nineteenth-century biscuit factory. Temporary art exhibitions often take up some of the gallery space, while the museum displays works by some of Portugal's most influential artists since the nineteenth century, along with foreign artists influenced by Portugal. Highlights include Almada Negreiros' 1920s panels from the old São Carlos cinema, showing Felix the Cat; a beautiful sculpture, *A Viúva* (*The Widow*), by António Teixeira Lopes; and some evocative early twentieth-century Lisbon scenes by water-colourist Carlos Botelho.

▼ SCULPTURE AT MUSEU DO CHIADO

Teatro Nacional de São Carlos

Rua Serpa Pinto 9 ☎ 213 468 408, ⓦ www.saocarlos.pt. Lisbon's main opera house, the Teatro Nacional de São Carlos, was built shortly after the original Lisbon opera house on Praça do Comércio was destroyed in the Great Earthquake. Heavily influenced by the leading Italian opera houses, it has a sumptuous Rococo interior, but you can only see it during performances of opera, ballet and classical music. You can enjoy the theatre's café-restaurant at other times, however, with pleasant outside tables.

Rua Garrett

Chiado's most famous street, Rua Garrett, is where you'll find some of the oldest shops and cafés in the city, as well as the **Igreja dos Mártires** (Church of the Martyrs) named after the English Crusaders who were killed during the siege of Lisbon. Some of the area's best shops can also be found in nearby Rua do Carmo, virtually rebuilt from scratch after the 1988 fire.

Shops

Ana Salazar

Rua do Carmo. One of Lisbon's best-known names for modern and individual designer clothes.

Armazéns do Chiado

Rua do Carmo 2. Daily 10am–10pm, restaurants until 11pm. This swish shopping centre sits on six floors above metro Baixa-Chiado in a structure that has risen from the ashes of the Chiado fire, though it retains its traditional facade. Various shops include branches of Massimo Duti (women),

▲ ARMAZÉNS DO CHIADO

Sportzone, Bodyshop and the classy toy shop Imaginarium. The top floor has a series of cafés and restaurants, including Brazilian chain *Chimarrão*, most offering great views.

Fábrica Sant'anna
Rua do Alecrim 95. If you're interested in Portuguese azulejos, check out this factory shop, founded in 1741, which sells copies of traditional designs and a great range of ceramics.

José Dias Sobral
Rua de São Paulo 218. Founded in 1880 and barely changed since, this traditional workshop at the foot of the Elevador da Bica sells quality leather belts, briefcases and shoe laces.

Livraria Bertrand
Rua Garrett 73. Portugal's oldest general bookshop, founded in 1773 and once the meeting place for Lisbon's literary set. With novels in English and a range of foreign magazines, it's also a good place to find English translations of Portuguese writers like Fernando Pessoa. Open daily.

Loja de Artesenato
Mercado da Ribeira, entrance on Avenida 24 de Julho. Upstairs in the market building, this shop specializes in art and crafts from Lisbon and the Tejo valley, with modern glassware, crafts and ceramics. Open daily.

Luvaria Ulisses
Rua do Carmo 87a. The superb, ornately-carved wooden doorway leads you into a minuscule glove shop, with hand-wear to suit all tastes tucked into rows of boxes.

Torres and Brinkmann
Rua Nova da Trindade 1b. The best place in the city to buy cookery equipment; it has stylish, high-quality pots, pans and utensils, including coffee-making gear and griddles. There's another branch just up the road at Trav. da Trindade 18–22, specializing in porcelain, glass and silverware.

Cafés

Bernard
Rua Garrett 104. Mon–Sat 8am–midnight. Often overlooked because of its proximity to *A Brasileira*, this ornate café offers superb cakes, ice cream and coffees; it also has an outdoor terrace on Chiado's most fashionable street.

A Brasileira

Rua Garrett 120. Daily 8am–2am.
Opened in 1905, and marked by
an outdoor bronze statue of the
poet Fernando Pessoa, this is the
most famous of Lisbon's old-
style coffee houses. The tables
on the pedestrianized street get
snapped up by tourists but the
real appeal is in its traditional
interior, where prices are
considerably cheaper than on
the outdoor esplanade, especially
if you stand at the long bar. At
night buskers often add a frisson
as the clientele changes to a
more youthful brigade, all on
the beer.

Café No Chiado

Largo do Picadeiro 11. Mon–Sat
11pm–2am. Tram #28 rattles past
this café-restaurant at the top
end of Rua Duque de Bragança,
with outdoor tables in a
picturesque square. There's
Internet access upstairs at *Ciber
Chiado*.

Café Vertigo

Travessa do Carmo 4 ☎213 433 112.
Daily 10am–midnight. An arty
crowd frequents this bar-brick
walled café with an ornate glass
ceiling. Occasional art exhibits
and a good range of cakes and
snacks.

Wagons-Lit

Estação Fluvial. Mon–Fri 7am–10pm,
Sat & Sun 7am–8.30pm. A simple
and tranquil spot with outdoor
tables facing the river, offering
inexpensive coffees, drinks and
snacks. A great place to while
away a few minutes if you have
a ferry or train to catch from
Cais do Sodré.

Restaurants

Associação Católica

Travessa do Ferragial 1. Mon–Fri
noon–3pm. There's no sign on
the door, but look for no. 1
on this small road just off Rua
do Ferragial and head to the
top floor for a self service
canteen offering a choice of
different dishes – from grilled
fish to large salads – each day.
The chief attractions are the
low prices and the rooftop
terrace with fine views over
the Tejo.

▼ SHOP SIGN, FÁBRICA SANTANNA

O Canteiro

Rua Vítor Cordon 8–10. Mon–Fri 7am–8pm. On a steep street served by tram #28, the cool, azulejo-covered interior harbours an inexpensive self-service counter feeding local workers with a fine range of dishes, like tuna and black-eyed bean salad or *bacalhau* rissoles, followed by fresh strawberries. It is particularly busy at lunchtime, when you may have to wait for a table.

Chez Degroote

Rua dos Duques de Bragança 4 ☎ 213 472 839. Mon–Sat noon–4pm & 7.30–11.30pm. Romantic spot in a tastefully renovated town house, with soaring ceilings and shuttered windows. Specialities include various beef dishes, omelettes and fish from around €9, with some delicious starters, too.

Comida da Ribeira

Mercado da Ribeira, entrance on Avenida 24 de Julho ☎ 210 312 600.

▼ TAVARES RICO

Daily noon–11pm. The market restaurant's buffets are so popular they lead to lunchtime scrums – come before 12.30pm to beat the rush. From €8, you can help yourself to hot and cold dishes including squid kebabs, *bacalhau* dishes, salads and *feijoada* (bean stew), though the à la carte menu is also good value, with mains from €9.

L'Entrecôte

Rua do Alecrim 117–120 ☎ 213 473 616. Mon–Fri 11.30am–3pm & 7pm–midnight, Sat & Sun 8pm–midnight. This upmarket, relaxing, wood-panelled restaurant with soaring ceilings has won awards for its entrecôte steak which is just as well, as that's all it serves. With a sauce said to contain 35 ingredients, it is truly delicious. There's also a good set menu for around €15. Dinner reservations are advised.

Porto de Abrigo

Rua dos Remolares 16–18 ☎ 213 460 873. Mon–Sat 9–11pm. This long-established and atmospheric restaurant near the main market serves good-value dishes such as octopus, salmon and *açorda de camarão* (shrimps with garlicky bread sauce).

Tavares Rico

Rua da Misericórdia 35 ☎ 213 421 112. Mon–Fri 12.30–3pm & 7.30–11pm, Sun 7.30–11pm. Gloriously ornate restaurant, one of Lisbon's oldest, dating from 1784. Dine in splendour on richly prepared lobster, duck or sole. Mains are from €25.

Bars

Bicaense

Rua da Bica Duarte Belo 38–42. Mon–Sat 12.30–3pm & 8pm–2am. Small, fashionable bar on the steep street used by the Elevador da Bica, with jazz and Latin sounds and a moderately priced bar-food menu.

British Bar

Rua Bernardino Costa 52 ☎ 213 422 367. Mon–Sat 8am–midnight.

Wonderful Anglo–Portuguese hybrid stuck in a 1930s time warp, featuring ceiling fans, marble counter and dark wooden shelves stacked with wines and spirits. There's also Guinness on tap and regulars who look as if they've been coming here since the day it opened.

Heróis

Calçada do Sacramento 14. Daily noon–2am.

Bright, white and minimalist split-level bar with a young, mixed crowd. Also serves decent nouveau Portuguese food.

Hotel Bairro Alto

Praça Luis de Camões 8 ☎ 213 408 223. Daily noon–midnight. Swish and stylish split-level hotel bar, with a giant triangular table in the main area, a downstairs video-room and laid-back lounge area full of comfy cushions. Pricey drinks come with generous bowls of nuts.

Vou ão Camões

Rua de Loreto 44. Tues–Sun 7–11pm.

All credit to the owners who have found space for tables on two floors of a bar barely larger than a broom cupboard. Attracts a clientele as quirky as the bar itself.

The Bairro Alto

The Bairro Alto, the upper town, sits solidly on a flat hill west of the Baixa. After the 1755 earthquake, this relatively unscathed district became the favoured residence of the aristocracy and the haunt of Lisbon's young bohemians. Home to the Institute of Art and Design and various designer boutiques, it is still the city's most fashionable district. By day, the quarter's grid of narrow, seventeenth-century streets feels essentially residential, with grocery stores open to the pavement and children playing in the cobbled streets. After dark, however, the area throngs with drinkers, clubbers and diners visiting its famed fado houses, bars, restaurants and shops. As a result, this is by far the best place in the city for an evening out. The most lively nightlife can be found in the tight grid of streets to the west of Rua da Misericórdia, particularly after midnight in Rua do Norte, Rua Diário de Notícias, Rua da Atalaia and Rua da Rosa. Running steeply downhill towards São Bento, Rua do Século is one of the area's most significantly historic streets. A sign at no. 89 marks the birthplace of the Marquês de Pombal, the minister responsible for rebuilding Lisbon after the Great Earthquake.

Elevador da Glória

Mon–Sat 7am–midnight, Sun 8am–midnight. €1.20. Everyone should ride the Elevador da Glória at least once to experience one of the city's most amazing feats of engineering. From the bottom of Calçada da Glória (off Praça dos Restauradores, see p.57), a funicular climbs the alarmingly sheer street in a couple of minutes, leaving the lower city behind as you ascend above its rooftops. Built in 1885, the tram system was originally powered by water displacement and then by steam, until electricity was introduced.

At the top of the Elevador da Glória, most people pause at the gardens, the **Miradouro de São Pedro de Alcântara**, from where there's a superb view across the city to the castle.

Igreja de São Roque

Largo de Trindade Coelha ☎213 235 381. Daily 8.30am–5pm. Free. The Igreja de São Roque stands in Largo Trindade Coelho, a square with a diminutive statue of a lottery seller. From the outside, this looks like the plainest church in the city, with a bleak Renaissance facade. However, inside lies an astonishing succession of side chapels, lavishly crafted with azulejos, multicoloured marble and Baroque painted ceilings.

The highlight is the **Capela de São João Baptista**, estimated for its size to be the most expensive chapel ever constructed. It was ordered

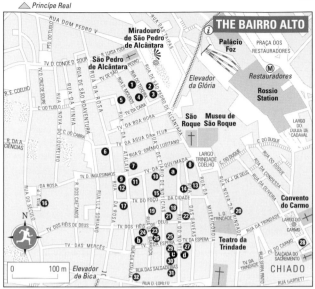

△ Princípe Real

THE BAIRRO ALTO ⓘ

Miradouro de São Pedro de Alcântara

Palácio Foz

PRAÇA DOS RESTAURADORES

São Pedro de Alcântara

Elevador da Glória

Restauradores

Ⓜ

Rossio Station

São Roque

Museu de São Roque

LARGO DO DUQUE DE CADAVAL

Convento do Carmo

Teatro da Trindade

CHIADO

Elevador de Bica

0 — 100 m

N

RESTAURANTS						LIVE MUSIC	
1° de Maio	32	Sinal Vermelho	14	Keops	6	Adega Machado	18
Águas do Bengo	4	3ul	30	Lisbona	5	Adega Mesquita	10
Bota Alta	11	**CAFES**		Portas Largas	9	Adega do Ribatejo	25
Brasuca	16	Leitaria Académica	28	Purex	31	A Severa	22
Calcuta	29	**BARS & CLUBS**		Sétimo Céu	23		
O Cantinho do Bem Estar	27			Solar do Vinho		**SHOPS**	
Cervejaria da Trindade	20	121	25	do Porto	3	Agencia Fake	a
Cravo e Canela	19	Arroz Doce	12	A Tasca	15	Eldorado	c
Gavéas	13	Bar Ártis	15	Tequila Bar	8	Espaço Fátima	
Olivier	1	Clube da Esquina	26	Tertúlia	21	Lopes	b
Pap'Açorda	17	Frágil	7	Ze dos Bois	24	Sneaker's Delight	d
A Primavera do Jerónimo	26	Harry's Bar	2				

from Rome in 1742 by Dom João V to honour his patron saint and, more dubiously, to gratify Pope Benedict XIV whom he had persuaded to confer a patriarchate on Lisbon. Designed using the most costly materials available, including ivory, agate, porphyry and lapis lazuli, it was erected at the Vatican for the Pope to celebrate Mass in, before being dismantled and shipped to Lisbon at the then vast cost of £250,000. If you take a close look at the four "oil paintings" of John the Baptist's life, you'll find that they are in fact

intricately worked mosaics. Today, the more valuable parts

▼ STATUE, LARGO TRINDADE COELHO

▲ CONVENTO DO CARMO RUINS

of the altar front are kept in the adjacent **museum** (Tues–Sun 10am–5pm; €1.50, free Sun 10am–2pm), which also displays sixteenth- to eighteenth-century paintings and the usual motley collection of church relics.

Convento do Carmo

Mon–Sat: April–Sept 10am–6pm; Oct–March 10am–5pm ☎213 478 629. €2.50. The pretty, enclosed Largo do Carmo holds the entrance to the ruined Convento do Carmo, whose beautiful Gothic arches rise grandly into the sky. Built between 1389 and 1423, and once the largest church in the city, it was semi-destroyed by the 1755 earthquake but is perhaps even more striking as a result. In the nineteenth century its shell was used as a chemical factory but today it houses the splendidly capricious **Museu Arqueológico do Carmo**, home to many of the treasures from monasteries that were dissolved after the 1834 Liberal revolution. The entire nave is open to the elements, with columns, tombs and statuary scattered in all corners. Inside, on either side of what was the main altar, are the main exhibits, centring on a series of tombs. Largest is the beautifully carved, two-metre-high stone tomb of Ferdinand I; nearby, that of Gonçalo de Sousa, chancellor to Henry the Navigator, is topped by a statue of Gonçalo himself, his clasped arms holding a book to signify his learning. Other noteworthy pieces include sixteenth-century Hispano-Arabic azulejos, an Egyptian sarcophagus (793–619 BC), whose inhabitant's feet are just visible underneath the lid; and, even more alarmingly, two pre-Columbian mummies which lie in glass cases, alongside the preserved heads of a couple of Peruvian Indians. Elsewhere there are arrowheads, prehistoric ceramics and coins dating back to the thirteenth century.

The exit to the **Elevador de Santa Justa** (see p.53) is at the side of the Convento do Carmo – go onto the rampway leading to it for fine views over the city.

Shops

Agencia Fake

Rua do Norte. Typical of the Bairro Alto: a designer clothes and shoe-shop that turns into a bar from early evening until 2am. Agencia 117, two doors down, has more clothes and doubles as a hair salon.

Eldorado

Rua do Norte 23–25. An interesting mixture of clubbing gear and secondhand cast-offs alongside old records and CDs, aimed at Lisbon's young groovers. A good place to head for if you need a

▲ NEWSAGENTS IN BAIRRO ALTO

new wardrobe for a night out without breaking the bank. Open until midnight.

Espaço Fátima Lopes

Rua da Atalaia 36. One of the few large shops in the Bairro Alto and flagship store for Lisbon's top designer. Her clothes are bold, colourful and confident, reflecting the current mood of many young Portuguese. She also runs a club in the basement, though seemingly only when she feels like it.

Sneaker's Delight

Rua do Norte 30–32. Pollock would be proud of the paint-spattered interior here, which displays a minimalist collection of very desirable, limited-edition trainers and shoes.

Cafés

Leitaria Académica

Largo do Carmo 1–3. Daily 7am–midnight. Outdoor tables on one of the city's leafiest squares, outside the ruined Carmo church. Besides drinks and snacks, it also does light lunches; in summer, the grilled sardines are hard to beat.

Restaurants

1° de Maio

Rua da Atalaia 8. Mon–Fri noon–3pm & 7–10.30pm, Sat 7–10.30pm.
Naked Chef-style food: simple slabs of grilled fish and meat with boiled veg and chips. You can watch the cook through a hatch at the back adding to the theatrics of a bustling, traditional *adega* (wine cellar) with a low, arched ceiling. Mains are around €10. Get there early to be sure of a table.

Águas do Bengo

Rua do Teixeira 1 ☎ 213 477 516. Mon–Sat 7.30pm–midnight. Owned by Angolan musician Waldemar Bastos, this African music bar-restaurant serves slightly pricey, tropically inspired dishes, from grilled fish to chicken stewed with palm oil. If Waldemar is in town and in the mood, he'll grab his guitar and play a tune or two. Reservations are advised. Usually closed in winter.

▲ CARD PLAYERS, LARGO DO CARMO

Bota Alta

Trav. da Queimada 37 ☎ 213 427 959.
Mon–Sat noon–2.30pm & 7–10.30pm.
Old tavern decorated with old
boots (*botas*) and an eclectic
picture collection. It attracts
queues for its vast portions of
sensibly priced traditional
Portuguese food – including
bacalhau com natas (cod cooked
in cream) – and jugs of local
wine. The tables are crammed in
and it's always packed; try to
arrive before 8pm or book in
advance.

Brasuca

Rua João Pereira da Rosa 7 ☎ 213 220
740. Daily noon–3pm & 7–10.30pm;
closed Mon Nov–April. Well-
established Brazilian restaurant
in a great old high-ceilinged
townhouse. Moderately priced
dishes include *feijoada moqueca*
(chicken and bean stew), *picanha*
(slices of garlicky beef) and lots
of other meaty choices.

Calcuta

Rua do Norte 17 ☎ 213 428 295. Mon–
Sat noon–3pm & 6.30–11pm. Very
popular Indian restaurant
attracting a youngish clientele.

▲ BOTA ALTA

Lots of chicken, seafood and
lamb curries, tandoori dishes,
and good vegetarian options.
Reservations are advised.

O Cantinho do Bem Estar

Rua do Norte 46. Tues–Sun 7–11pm.
The decor borders on
Portuguese kitsch, with ceramic
chickens and over-the-top rural
furnishings, but the "canteen of
well-being" lives up to its name.
Service is friendly and, from the
menu, the rice dishes and
generous salads are the best bet;
the passable house wine is
served in ceramic jugs.

Cervejaria da Trindade

Rua Nova da Trindade 20 ☎ 213 423
506. Daily 9am–2am. The city's
oldest beer-hall dates from 1836.
At busy times you'll be shown
to your table; at others, try and
avoid the dull modern
extensions and find a space in
the original vaulted hall,
decorated with some of the
city's loveliest azulejos, depicting
the elements and seasons.
Shellfish is the speciality, though
the other fish and meat dishes
are lighter on the wallet. There
is also a patio garden and – a
rarity – a children's menu.
Highchairs can be supplied.

Gáveas

Rua das Gáveas 82–84 ☎ 213 426
460. Mon–Fri noon–3pm & 7.30–
11.30pm, Sat & Sun 7.30–11.30pm.
Good-value if spartan *adega*
(wine cellar) with reliable dishes
of the day and a long menu
featuring pasta, *açorda*, meats and
bacalhau.

Olivier

Rua do Teixeira 35 ☎ 213 421 024
ⓦ www.restaurante.olivier.com.
Mon–Sat 8pm–2am The most
talked-about restaurant amongst
Lisbon foodies with an

excellent-value set menu of €30 offering quality new Portuguese cuisine. Expect starters such as cherry tomato kebabs with feta, crab guacamole or game sausage; mains like *scallops a la creme* or roast pork with honey and rosemary; and divine desserts including chocolate *coulant* with ice cream and fruit *coulis*. Reservations are recommended.

Pap'Açorda

Rua da Atalaia 57–59 ☎213 464 811. Tues–Sat 12.30–2pm & 8–11.30pm. Renowned restaurant that attracts Lisbon's fashionable elite to its chandelier-hung dining room, converted from an old bakery. *Açorda* is the house speciality, served with seafood. There are also regional dishes (including lamprey and fried goat) and fine starters such as oysters or tiger prawns. Mains start at €15. Reservations are advised.

A Primavera do Jerónimo

Trav. da Espera 34 ☎213 420 477. Mon–Sat noon–3pm & 7–11pm. This tiny place neatly crams in a couple of dozen diners, a bar, kitchen area and a very long menu, overseen by the owner and his daughter. Azulejos inscribed with Portuguese proverbs dot the walls, while the mid-priced, home-cooked Portuguese dishes are highly rated (as newspaper reviews on the walls testify). Portions aren't huge by local standards but the crisp-like fried potatoes are a hit. Reservations are advised.

Sinal Vermelho

Rua das Gáveas 89 ☎213 461 252. Mon–Sat 12.30–2.30pm & 7.30–11.30pm; closed July. Roomy *adega* (wine cellar) that's popular with Lisbon's moneyed youth. Specialities include well-

▲ NIGHTLIFE IN BAIRRO ALTO

presented *açorda de gambas* (prawns in garlicky bread sauce) and *arroz de polvo* (octopus rice) and there's an impressive wine list. It is best to book ahead.

Sul

Rua do Norte 13 ☎213 462 445. Tues–Sun noon–2am. Jazzy, split-level wine bar and restaurant – the round table in the lower mezzanine is ideal for large groups. Dishes include chicken kebabs, risotto and *bife na pedra* (steak cooked on a stone). Mains start at around €16.

Bars and clubs

121

Rua do Norte 117–119. Tues–Sat 7pm–3.30am. Laid-back lounge bar with low, comfy seats, aboriginal art and ambient sounds; the TVs in the corner rather spoil the effect though.

Arroz Doce

Rua da Atalaia 117–119 ☎213 462 601. Mon–Sat 6pm–4am. An unpretentious bar in the middle of the frenetic Bairro Alto nightlife, with friendly owners; try "Auntie's" sangria, poured from a jug the size of a house.

Bar Ártis

Rua do Diário de Notícias 95 ℗ 213 424 795. Tues–Fri 8.30pm–2am, Sat & Sun 8.30pm–4am. A laid-back jazz bar with arty posters on the wall and marble table-tops. It's popular with creative types, who usually spend a night here in animated conversation over a few bottles of its excellent *vinho*. Also does a fine range of snacks, like chicken *tostas* (toasted sandwiches).

Clube da Esquina

Rua da Barroca 30 ℗ 213 427 149. Daily 4.30pm–2am. Buzzing little corner bar with ancient radios on the walls and DJs spinning discs. Attracts a young crowd enjoying vast measures of spirits.

Frágil

Rua da Atalaia 126 ℗ 213 469 578, ⓦ www.fragil.com. Mon–Sat 11pm–4am. This has long been one of Lisbon's most popular clubs, and it remains very lively, particularly from Thursday to Saturday, though it doesn't really get going until after 1am. It's partly gay, definitely pretentious and has a strict door policy (it helps if you're young and beautiful). Music is house and techno. You'll need to ring the bell to get in.

Harry's Bar

Rua de São Pedro de Alcântara 57–61 ℗ 213 460 760. Daily 10pm–6am. A tiny front-room bar with waiter service, tasty bar snacks and fado sounds. It's frequented by an eclectic clientele. Ring the bell for admission.

Keops

Rua da Rosa 157–159 ℗ 213 428 773. Mon–Sat 10pm–3.30am. Friendly bar, playing everything from Moby to Madonna. The doors are thrown open to the street, while the candlelit interior enhances the laid-back atmosphere.

Lisbona

Rua da Atalaia 196 ℗ 213 471 412. Mon–Sat 7pm–2am. Earthy bar attracting its fair share of local characters and Bairro Alto trendies. Decor is basic – chequerboard tiles covered in soccer memorabilia, old film posters and graffiti – but there's catchy pop music and good beer.

Portas Largas

Rua da Atalaia 105 ℗ 218 466 379. Daily 8pm–2am. The bar's *portas largas* (big doors) are usually thrown wide open, inviting the neighbourhood into this friendly black-and-white-tiled *adega* (wine cellar). There are cheapish drinks, music from fado to pop, and a young, mixed gay and straight clientele, which spills onto the streets on warm evenings before hitting *Frágil*, just over the road.

▲ CLUBE DA ESQUINA

▲ TERTÚLIA

Purex

Rua das Salgadeiras 28. Tues–Sun 11pm–4am. This small and friendly dance bar, popular with lesbians but not exclusively so, offers ambient music on Tuesdays and Wednesdays, and more upbeat sounds – guaranteed to fill the small dance floor – on Thursday to Sunday nights.

Sétimo Céu

Trav. da Espera 54 ☎ 213 466 471. Mon–Sat 10pm–2am. An obligatory stop for gays and lesbians, who imbibe beers and *caipirinhas* served by the Brazilian owner. The great atmosphere spills out onto the street.

Solar do Vinho do Porto

Rua de São Pedro de Alcântara 45 ☎ 213 475 707, ⦿ www.ivp.pt. Mon–Sat 2pm–midnight. Firmly on the tourist circuit, the Port Wine Institute is set in the eighteenth-century Palácio Ludovice. The Institute, based in the northern city of Porto, regulates and promotes the production of port wine. It opened its Lisbon headquarters here in 1944 and now lures in visitors with over three hundred types of port, starting at around €2 a glass and rising to some €25 for a glass of forty-year-old J.W. Burmester. Drinks are served at low tables in a comfortable old eighteenth-century mansion. The waiters are notoriously snooty and the cheaper ports never seem to be in stock, but it's still a good place to kick off an evening.

A Tasca Tequila Bar

Trav. da Queimada 13–15. Daily 11.30am–2am. Colourful Mexican bar with Latin sounds, which caters to a good-time crowd downing tequilas, margaritas and Brazilian *caipirinhas*.

Tertúlia

Rua do Diário de Notícias 60 ☎ 213 462 704. Mon–Thurs 8.30pm–3am, Fri & Sat 8.30pm–4am. Relaxed café-bar with inexpensive drinks, newspapers to browse, background jazz and varied art exhibitions that change every couple of weeks. There's a piano for customers, too, in case you get the urge to play.

Ze dos Bois

Rua da Barroca 59 ⊕213 430 205 ⓦwww.zedebois.org. Fri & Sat 11pm–2am. Rambling art venue that hosts various installations, arthouse films and exhibitions (hours vary – phone for details) along with occasional concerts. At weekends, local DJs showcase their talents to a bohemian crowd.

Live music

Adega Machado

Rua do Norte 91 ⊕213 224 640. Tues–Sun 8.30pm–3am. Beautiful music-themed tiles mark the entrance to one of the longest-established Bairro Alto fado houses, offering fado from both Lisbon and Coimbra. A minimum charge of €16 builds to at least €25 a head if you sample the fine Portuguese cooking.

Adega Mesquita

Rua do Diário de Notícias 107 ⊕213 219 280 ⓦwww.adegamesquita.com. Daily 8pm–1.30am. Another of the big Bairro Alto fado houses, featuring better-than-average music and traditional folk dancing and singing, though tourists make up the bulk of the clientele. Main courses cost from €18.

Adega do Ribatejo

Rua do Diário de Notícias 23 ⊕213 468 343. Mon–Sat noon–midnight. This great little *adega* (wine cellar) is a favoured haunt for British artists Gilbert and George. It's popular with locals, too, who describe the fado (from 8.30pm nightly) here as "pure emotion". The singers include a couple of professionals, the manager and – best of all – the cooks. Also has one of the lowest minimum charges (around €10) and delicious, inexpensive food.

A Severa

Rua das Gáveas 51–57 ⊕213 464 006 ⓦwww.asevera.com. Mon–Wed & Fri–Sun 9.30pm–1am. A city institution, named after the nineteenth-century singer Maria Severa. The club attracts big fado names and equally large prices. Minimum consumption of €19 builds to more like €30 with food (served until midnight).

Praça do Príncipe Real and around

North of the tight Bairro Alto grid, the streets open out around the leafy Praça do Príncipe Real, one of the city's loveliest squares. Laid out in 1860 and surrounded by the ornate homes of former aristocrats – now largely turned into offices – the square is the focal point of Lisbon's best gay nightclubs, though by day it is largely populated by children in the local play park and locals playing cards under the trees. The square also shelters a surprising underground museum, and is a short walk from the well-hidden but extensive botanical gardens.

Museu da Água Príncipe Real

Mon–Sat 10am–6pm. €1.50. The square's central pond and fountain are built over a covered reservoir that houses the Museu da Água Príncipe Real. Steps lead down inside the eerie nineteenth-century reservoir, where you can admire brick and vaulted ceilings, part of a network of underground water supplies that link up with the Aqueduto das Águas Livres (see p.124). One of the tunnels from this reservoir heads down through what is now the *Enoteca* wine bar (see p.102). The museum also hosts occasional temporary art exhibits that you admire from a series of walkways winding among the columns, usually accompanied by ambient music.

Museu da Ciência and Museu da História Natural

The museums of science and natural history are housed in a nineteenth-century Neoclassical former technical college. The Museu da Ciência (Mon–Fri 10am–1pm & 2–5pm, Sat 3–6pm; closed Aug; €2.50) has some absorbing geological exhibits and a low-tech interactive section where you can balance balls on jets of air and swing pendulums among throngs of school kids.
The Museu da Historia Natural opposite (Mon–Fri 10am–1pm & 2–3pm; closed Aug; free), houses a rather dreary collection of stuffed animals, eggs and shells, though temporary exhibitions can be more diverting.

Jardim Botânico

Rua Escola Politécnica ☎ 213 921 830
ⓦ www.jb.vl.pt. May–Oct Mon–Fri

▼ CATEDRAL DO PÃO

△ Rato

PRAÇA DO PRÍNCIPE REAL

0   100 m

Museu de História
Natural & Museu
da Ciência

Jardim Botânico

Universidade
Internacional

RESTAURANTS
Comida de Santo   3
Esplanada   5
Faz Frio   7
Mal Amanhado   1
Tascardoso   8

CAFÉS
Catedral do Pão   9
Pão de Canela   12

Academia das
Ciências de Lisboa

SHOP
Solar Albuquerque   a

BARS & CLUBS
106   14
Bric-a-Brac Bar   6
Enoteca   4
Finalmente   13
Max   15
Pavilhão Chinês   10
Snob   11
Trumps   2

9am–8pm, Sat & Sun 10am–6pm;
Nov–April Mon–Fri 9am–6pm, Sat &
Sun 10am–6pm. €3. These
nineteenth-century botanical
gardens are almost entirely
invisible from the surrounding
streets and provide a tranquil
escape from the city bustle. The
Portuguese explorers
introduced many plant species
to Europe during the Golden
Age of exploration (from the
fifteenth to eighteenth
centuries) and these gardens,
laid out between 1858 and
1878, are packed with twenty
thousand neatly labelled species
from around the world. Steep,
shady paths lead downhill
under towering palms and
luxuriant shrubs.

Shops

Solar Albuquerque
Rua Dom Pedro V 66–72. A huge
treasure trove of antique tiles,
plates and ceramics – great for a
browse.

Cafés

Catedral do Pão
Rua Dom Pedro V 57c. Daily 7am–
7.30pm. Relaxed corner
café-bakery with a wonderfully
ornate high ceiling, where you
can have coffee and croissants at
the counter or buy fresh pastries
to take away.

Pão de Canela

Praça das Flôres 27–28. Mon–Fri 7.30am–11pm, Sat & Sun 8am–11pm. Tastefully modernized, tile-fronted café serving great pastries, soups and snacks. The outdoor terrace faces a children's play area on this lovely square.

Restaurants

Comida de Santo

Calçada Engenheiro Miguel Pais 39 ☎ 213 963 339. Daily 12.30–3.30pm & 7.30pm–1am. Rowdy, late-opening and pricey Brazilian restaurant serving cocktails and classic dishes such as *feijoada a brasileira* (Brazilian bean stew). Reservations are advised.

Esplanada

Praça do Príncipe Real ☎ 962 311 669. Daily 8am–midnight. A good range of pizzas, tortilla, quiches and rustic wholemeal sandwiches make this an ideal and inexpensive lunch spot. The outdoor tables set under the trees get snapped up quickly,

though the glass pavilion comes into its own when the weather turns. It's also a popular gay haunt.

Faz Frio

Rua Dom Pedro V 96–98 ☎ 213 461 860. Daily 9am–midnight; usually closed late Aug–late Sept. A traditional restaurant, replete with coloured tiles and confessional-like cubicles. The huge portions of *bacalhau*, seafood paella and prawns in breadcrumbs are good value, as are a variety of dishes of the day. Dinner reservations are advised, especially at the weekend.

Mal Amanhado

Rua Alegria 54A ☎ 213 433 381. Mon–Fri noon–3pm & 7.30pm–2am, Sat 7.30pm–2am. Steeply downhill towards Avenida da Liberdade, this bustling local serves superb dishes such as *migas* (meat or fish in a bready garlic sauce), mixed fried fish and pork kebabs from around €10. Recommended.

Tascardoso

Rua Dom Pedro V 137 ☎ 213 427 578. Mon–Fri noon–3pm & 7–8pm. Go through the stand-up bar and down the stairs to the tiny eating area for excellent and inexpensive tapas-style meats and cheeses and good-value hot dishes.

Bars and clubs

106

Rua São Marçal 106 ☎ 213 427 373. Daily 9pm–2am. Ring on the doorbell to gain entry to this friendly gay bar which makes a good place to start the evening. Fridays are often leather nights.

▲ COFFEE AND *PASTEL DE NATA*

Bric-a-Brac Bar

Rua Cecílio de Sousa 82–84 ☎213 428 971. Wed–Mon 11pm–4am. On a steep road beyond Praça do Príncipe Real, this cruisy gay disco has a large dance floor, a dark room and various bars. Occasional drag shows also feature.

Enoteca

Rua da Mãe de Agua ☎213 422 079. Tues–Sun 6pm–2am. This extraordinary wine bar is set in the bowels of a nineteenth-century bathhouse whose underground tunnels once piped water into Lisbon. The bar offers a long list of Portuguese wines, which you can enjoy with regional breads and assorted *petiscos* (snacks) such as oysters or dates with bacon. It gets busy at weekends so it's best to reserve if you want to eat, though you can always squeeze in for a drink or sit at one of the outside tables.

▲ ENOTECA WINE BAR

a pool room. Most are completely lined with mirrored cabinets containing a bizarre range of artefacts from around the world, including a cabinet of model trams. There's waiter service and the usual drinks are supplemented by a long list of exotic cocktails.

Finalmente

Rua da Palmeira 38 ☎213 479 923. Daily midnight–4am. A first-class gay disco with lashings of kitsch, famed for its drag shows (at 2am) featuring skimpily dressed young *senhoritas* camping it up to high-tech sounds.

Max

Rua São Marçal 15 ☎213 952 726 Daily 10pm–2am. Cosy gay bar increasingly popular amongst bears, with occasional strip shows.

Pavilhão Chinês

Rua Dom Pedro V 89 ☎213 424 729. Mon–Sat 6pm–2am, Sun 9pm–2am. Once a nineteenth-century tea and coffee merchants' shop, this is now a quirky bar set in a series of comfy rooms, including

Snob

Rua do Século 178 ☎213 463 723. Daily 4.30pm–3am. Cosy and upmarket bar and restaurant, full of media types enjoying cocktails. It's a good late-night option which also serves inexpensive steaks or light snacks.

Trumps

Rua da Imprensa Nacional 104b ☎213 971 059. Tues–Sun midnight–6am. Popular gay disco with a reasonably relaxed door policy. It's a bit cruisy during the middle of the week, and it gets packed from Thursday to Saturday, when there's also a high lesbian turnout. Drag shows are held on Wednesdays and Sundays.

São Bento, Santos, Estrela and Lapa

São Bento is home to the impressive Palácio da Assembléia, Portugal's parliamentary building. The area also houses some good ethnic restaurants, a legacy of the city's first black community who were originally slaves, brought back by the often brutal maritime traders. Beyond São Bento is the leafy district of Estrela, best known for its gardens and enormous basilica. To the south lies the opulent suburb of Lapa, Lisbon's diplomatic quarter, sheltering some of its top hotels. Sumptuous mansions peer out majestically towards the Tejo, whilst grand embassy buildings line the Rua do Sacramento à Lapa. The Museu Nacional de Arte Antiga below here is Portugal's national gallery, while down on the riverfront, Santos is being promoted as "the district of design" with some of the city's coolest shops and bars and a new Norman Foster hotel, which will be opening in a couple of years.

Palácio da Assembléia

The late sixteenth-century Neoclassical facade of the Palácio da Assembléia was originally that of the Mosteiro de São Bento, a Benedictine monastery, which the government took over in 1834 after the abolition of religious orders. Today it is the parliament building; it's not open to the public, though if you have an interest you can arrange a tour by special arrangement (☎213 919 000). Most visitors make do with the view of its steep white steps from tram #28 as it rattles along Calçada da Estrela.

Casa Museu Amália Rodrigues

Rua de São Bento 193 ☎213 971 896. Tues–Sun 10am–1pm & 2–6pm. €5.
The daughter of an Alfama orange-seller, Amália Rodrigues was the undisputed queen of fado music until her death in 1999, which instigated three days of national mourning. The house where she lived since the 1950s has been kept as it was, and you can also admire original posters advertising her performances on stage and in the cinema.

Basílica and Jardim da Estrela

Igreja daily 8.30am–12.30pm & 3–7.30pm. Free. Tram #28 or 25.
The impressive Basílica da Estrela is a vast monument to late-eighteenth-century Neoclassicism. Constructed by order of Queen Maria I (whose tomb lies within), and completed in 1790, its landmark white dome can be seen from much of the city. Opposite is the Jardim da Estrela, one of the city's

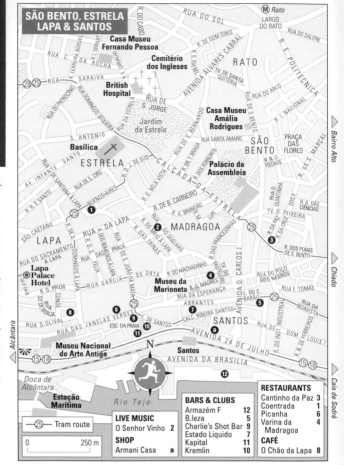

SÃO BENTO, ESTRELA LAPA & SANTOS

LIVE MUSIC	
O Senhor Vinho	2

SHOP	
Armani Casa	a

BARS & CLUBS	
Armazém F	12
B.leza	5
Charlie's Shot Bar	9
Estado Liquido	7
Kapital	11
Kremlin	10

RESTAURANTS	
Cantinho da Paz	3
Coentrada	1
Picanha	6
Varina da Madragoa	4

CAFÉ	
O Chão da Lapa	8

Tram route ⓐ — 25

0   250 m

most enjoyable gardens; it is a quiet refuge with a pond-side café, a well-equipped children's playground and even a library kiosk for those who fancy absorbing a spot of Portuguese literature under the palms.

Cemitério dos Ingleses

The name translates as "The English Cemetery" (ring loudly for entry) but it is actually a cemetery for all Protestants, founded in 1717. Here, among the cypresses and tombs of various expatriates, lie the remains of Henry Fielding, author of *Tom Jones*. He came to Lisbon hoping the climate would improve his failing health, but his inability to recuperate may have influenced his verdict on Lisbon as "the nastiest city in the world".

Casa Museu Fernando Pessoa

Rua Coelho da Rocha 16 ☎ 213 968 190. Mon–Wed & Fri 10am–6pm, Thurs

1–8pm. Free. Tram #28 or 25. This unassuming house is where Portugal's most celebrated modern writer, Fernando Pessoa, lived for the last fifteen years of his life. The heavily restored interior contains a few of Pessoa's personal belongings, including his diaries. There are also exhibitions of works by artists influenced by Pessoa, a library of his own works, and Almada Negreiros's famous painting of the writer with his distinctive spectacles (themselves on display in the museum) and black hat.

▲ ESTRELA BASILICA AND TRAM # 25

Museu Nacional de Arte Antiga

Rua das Janelas Verdes 95 ☎ 213 912 800, ⓦ www.mnarteantiga-ipmuseus.pt. Tues 2–6pm, Wed–Sun 10am–6pm. €3. Bus #40, #60, #27 or #49. The Museu Nacional de Arte Antiga features the largest collection of Portuguese fifteenth- and sixteenth-century paintings in the country, European art from the fourteenth century to the present day and a rich display of applied art. All of this is well-exhibited in a tastefully converted seventeenth-century palace, once owned by the Marquês de Pombal. The museum highlights ten "reference points" to guide you round the extensive collection. The prinicipal highlight is Nuno Gonçalves's altarpiece dedicated to St Vincent (1467–70), a brilliantly marshalled composition depicting Lisbon's patron saint receiving homage from all ranks of its citizens, their faces appearing remarkably modern. The other main highlight is Hieronymus Bosch's stunningly gruesome *Temptation of St Anthony* in room 57 (don't miss the image on the back of the painting, showing the arrest of Christ). Elsewhere, seek out the altar panel depicting the *Resurrection* by Raphael; Francisco de Zurbarán's *The Twelve Apostles;* a small statue of a nymph by Auguste Rodin and works by Albrecht Dürer, Cranach, Fragonard and Josefa de Óbidos, who is considered one of Portugal's greatest female painters.

The Oriental art collection shows how the Portuguese were influenced and inspired by Indian, African and Oriental designs derived from the trading links of the sixteenth century. There is inlaid furniture from Goa, Turkish and Syrian azulejos, Qing Dynasty porcelain and a fantastic series of late sixteenth-century Japanese *namban* screens (room 14), depicting the Portuguese landing at Nagasaki. The Japanese regarded the Portuguese traders as southern barbarians (*namban*) with large noses – hence their Pinocchio-like features. The palace was built over the remains of the sixteenth-century St Albert monastery, most of which was razed during the 1755 earthquake, although its beautiful chapel can still be seen today, downstairs by the main entrance. Don't miss the café, situated in the attractive formal gardens overlooking the Tejo.

Museu da Marioneta
Rua da Esperança 146 ☎213 942 810. Wed–Sun 10am–1pm & 2–6pm. €2.50 (children €1.50).
Contemporary and historical puppets from around the world are displayed in this former eighteenth-century convent and demonstrated in a well laid-out

museum. Highlights include shadow puppets from Turkey and Indonesia, string marionettes, Punch and Judy-style puppets and almost life-sized faintly disturbing contemporary figures by Portuguese puppeteer Helena Vaz, which are anything but cute. There are also video displays and projections, while the final room exhibits Wallace and Gromit-style plasticine figures with demonstrations on how they are manipulated for films.

Shops

Armani Casa
Largo de Santos 15c. Designer interior store with stylish furniture, accessories and linen, one of several clustered round the leafy Largo de Santos. *Paris Sete* at #14d sells similar fare.

Cafés

O Chão da Lapa
Rua de Olival 8–9. Daily 9am–7.30pm. Sophisticated tea rooms with comfy banquettes, mirrors and gilt fittings. The various snacks include croissants, scones and cakes.

Restaurants

Cantinho da Paz
Rua da Paz 4 ☎213 969 698. Daily 12.30–2.30pm & 3.30–11pm. Though favoured by MPs from the parliament building, this is an unpretentious Goan restaurant just off tram route #28. Reservations are advised since it's only small. There's shark soup, prawn curry and a

▼ VIEW FORM LAPA STREET

few vegetarian options on offer, served in a homely little dining room overseen by an enthusiastic owner who can guide you through the well-priced menu.

Coentrada

Rua de São Domingos à Lapa 100 ☎213 928 860. Mon–Fri noon–3pm. Set in the former Palácio dos Condes de Monte, this stylish restaurant serves quality Portuguese lunches. Tables are also set out in the lovely old courtyard surrounded by azulejos and below the palace bell tower.

Picanha

Rua das Janelas Verdes 47 ☎213 975 401. Mon–Fri 12.45–3pm & 7.45–11.30pm, Sat & Sun 7.45–11.30pm. This ornately tiled restaurant specializes in *picanha* (strips of beef in garlic sauce) accompanied by black-eyed beans, salad and potatoes. Great if this appeals to you, since for a fixed-price of €13.50 you can eat as much of the stuff as you want; otherwise forget it, as it's all that's on offer. Reservations are advised.

Varina da Madragoa

Rua das Madres 34 ☎213 965 533. Tues–Fri 12.45–3.30pm & 7.45–11.30pm, Sat 7.45–11.30pm. Once the haunt of the Nobel Prize for Literature winner, José Saramago, and it's easy to see why he liked it: a lovely, traditional restaurant with grape-motif azulejos on the walls and a menu featuring superb dishes such as *bacalhau*, trout and steaks. Desserts include a splendid almond ice cream with hot chocolate sauce.

Bars and clubs

Armazém F

Rua da Cintura, Armazém 65 ☎213 220 160 ⓦwww.armazemf.com. Thurs–Sun 8.30pm–5am. Brazilian bar and club on the riverfront at Cais do Gás, though dancing is more the norm than gassing. There's a reasonably relaxed door policy and a mix of live pop bands and resident DJs playing house and samba. It attracts a young, lively and partly Brazilian crowd.

B.leza

Largo Conde de Barão 50 ☎213 963 735. Wed–Sat 11.30pm–4am. There's live African music most nights in this wonderful sixteenth-century building, with plenty of space to dance, tables to relax at, and Cape Verdean food.

Charlie's Shot Bar

Rua das Janelas Verdes 2. Mon–Sat 9pm–2am. A great place to kick-start an evening, with a comprehensive menu of exotic cocktails mixed by the friendly bar staff. Arrive early to grab a space at the bar as it gets packed at weekends.

Estado Liquido

Largo de Santos 5A ☎213 955 820 ⓦwww.estadoliquido.com Sun–Thurs 8pm–2am, Fri & Sat 8pm–4am. Right on Santos' main square, this bar and club has a roomy feel despite its popularity with a young crowd lured by the prominent club DJs. Easy-going door policy and efficient service. Minimum consumption is around €10.

Kapital

Avda 24 de Julho 68 ☎213 955 963. Mon & Sun 10.30pm–4am, Tues–Sat 10.30pm–6am. Long-established venue, with three sleekly designed floors full of bright young things buying expensive drinks and dancing to techno. It can be hard work getting past the style police on the door but there's a great rooftop terrace once you're in.

Kremlin

Escadinhas da Praia 5 ☎216 087 768. Tues–Sat midnight–10am. The tough door policy, based on its reputation as one of the city's most fashionable nightspots, has put off many old-hand clubbers. However, it's still packed with flash, young, raving Lisboetas. It's best to come after 2am.

▲ KREMLIN CLUB

Live Music

O Senhor Vinho

Rua do Meio à Lapa 18 ☎213 972 681. Mon–Sat 8.30pm–2.30am. In the fashionable Madragoa district, this famous fado club has a relaxed atmosphere. It features some of the best singers in Portugal, which means high prices; usually around €50 a head. Reservations are advised.

Alcântara and the docks

Loomed over by the enormous Ponte 25 de Abril suspension bridge, Alcântara has a decidedly industrial hue, with a tangle of flyovers and cranes from the docks dominating the skyline. Nevertheless, the area is well known for its nightlife, thanks mainly to its dockside warehouse conversions that shelter cafés, restaurants and clubs. Parts of Alcântara are also getting a makeover under eminent French architect Jean Nouve; the area should see some ambitious ultra-modern residential and commercial buildings to complement an enlarged cruise terminal.

Doca de Alcântara

The Doca de Alcântara remains the city's main docks with luxury cruise ships calling daily. By day, the dock's main attraction is the **Dom Fernando II e Glória** frigate (☎213 620 010; Tues–Sun 10am–5pm; €3), built in India in 1843 and now a museum showing what life at sea was like in the mid-nineteenth century. After dark, the boat-bars and warehouse conversions come into their own; its clubs and bars attract an older, more moneyed crowd than those of the Bairro Alto.

Doca de Santo Amaro

Just west of the Doca de Alcântara lies the more intimate Doca de Santo Amaro, nestling right under the humming traffic and rattling trains crossing Ponte 25 de Abril. This small, almost completely enclosed marina is filled with bobbing sailing boats and lined with tastefully converted warehouses. Its international cafés and restaurants are pricier than usual

▼ ALCÂNTARA DOCK

△ Parque de Monsanto

ALCÂNTARA & THE DOCKS

0   250 m

N

CAMPO DE OURIQUE

ALCÂNTARA

Cemitéria dos Prazeres

Alcântara

Tapada das Necessidades

Palácio das Necessidades

Museu do C.C. e Cultural de Macau

Museu de Arte Antiga

Alcântara Mar

Doca de Alcântara

Don Fernando II e Gloria

Lisbon Congress Centre

Estação Marítima

Doca de Santo Amaro

Gare Marítima de Alcântara

RESTAURANTS		BARS & CLUBS	
Alcântara Café	1	Blues Café	3
Cosmos Café	7	Buddah Bar	11
Espalha Brasas	10	Doca de Santo	4
Tertúlia do Tejo	8	Havana	5
		Op Art	12

		CAFÉ	
Queens	2	Zonadoca	9
Speakeasy	6		

—⑱— Tram route

▽ Caparica

---

for Lisbon but the constant comings and goings of the Tejo provide plenty of free entertainment. Leaving Doca de Santo Amaro at its western side, you can pick up a pleasant riverside path that leads all the way to Belém (see p.114), twenty minutes' walk away.

Museu do Centro Científico e Cultural de Macau

Rua da Junqueira 30 ☏ 213 617 570. Tues–Sat 10am–5pm, Sun noon–6pm. €3. This attractively laid-out museum is dedicated to Portugal's historical trading links with the Orient and, specifically, its former colony of Macao,

which was handed back to Chinese rule in 1999. There are model boats and audio displays detailing early sea voyages, as well as various historic journals and artefacts, including a seventeenth-century portable wooden altar, used by travelling clergymen. Upstairs, exhibitions of Chinese art from the sixteenth to the nineteenth centuries show off ornate collections of porcelain, silverware and applied art, most notably an impressive array of opium pipes and ivory boxes.

Ponte 25 de Abril

Resembling the Golden Gate

bridge in San Francisco, the hugely impressive Ponte 25 de Abril was opened in 1966 as a vital link between Lisbon and the southern banks of the Tejo. Around 2.3km in length, the main bridge rises to 70m above the river, though its main pillars are nearly 200m tall. It was originally named Ponte de Salazar after the dictatorial prime minister who ruled Portugal with an iron fist from 1932 to 1968, but took its present name to mark the date of the revolution that overthrew Salazar's regime in 1974. You'll pass over it if you take a bus or train south of the Tejo (see p.159).

Cafés

Zonadoca

Pavilhão 7a, Doca de Santo Amaro. Mon & Wed–Sun 12.30pm–2am. Worth a visit for its ice cream alone, though you can also enjoy coffee or alcoholic drinks at this friendly, family-oriented café – with life-sized models of Laurel and Hardy and other celebrities for company.

Restaurants

Alcântara Café

Rua Maria Luísa Holstein 15 ☎213 637 176. Daily 8pm–3am. Stunning, if pricey, designer bar-restaurant, blending industrial steel pillars with stylish decor. The food on offer includes prawns in lemon sauce, goat's cheese salad and an array of fish dishes. This is a place to be seen before moving on to the neighbouring

clubs, hence the high prices. Reservations are advised.

Cosmos Café

Armazém 15, Doca de Santo Amaro ☎213 972 747. Daily noon–4am. Relatively inexpensive for these parts, with pasta, pizza or salads from around €8, and plenty of outside seating facing the marina. After midnight, the interior becomes a dance floor until the small hours.

Espalha Brasas

Armazém 12, Doca de Santo Amaro ☎213 962 059. Mon–Sat noon–4am. Superb if expensive grilled meats and fish can be enjoyed at the outdoor riverside tables, or head for the bright upstairs room, which offers great views over the river. Daily specials are from around €12.

Tertúlia do Tejo

Pavilhão 1, Doca de Santo Amaro ☎213 955 552. Daily 12.30–3pm & 7.30pm–midnight. Upmarket Portuguese restaurant, housed on three floors of a converted warehouse. There are evocative old photos of Portugal in the upstairs room and more intimate seating in the attic, plus fine river views from all floors. The

▼ FISHING BY THE PONTE 25 DE ABRIL

flavoured vodkas are a hit, too. Reservations are advised.

Bars and clubs

Blues Café
Rua da Cintura do Porto de Lisboa ☎213 957 085. Tues–Thurs 8pm–4am, Fri & Sat 8pm–5am. Lisbon's only blues club occupies a converted dockside warehouse. There's pricey Cajun food served in the restaurant until 12.30am, live music on Mondays and Thursdays, and club nights with the latest dance music on Fridays and Saturdays from 2.30am. Don't be put off by the advertised minimum consumption of €150, more of a ploy to put off the hoi polloi than a legal requirement.

Buddah Bar
Gare Marítima de Alcântara ☎213 950 555 ⓦwww.buddha.com.pt. Wonderful eastern-influenced bar and club housed in a 1940s maritime station, inspired by the Paris original. There are many chillout areas upstairs, most with an "opium den" feel, with a big dance floor downstairs. Smart dress is recommended, and check opening hours in advance as it's sometimes booked for private functions. At other times, there's a minimum consumption of around €20 (men) and €10 (women).

Doca de Santo
Doca de Santo Amaro ☎213 963 535. Mon–Thurs 12.30pm–1am, Fri–Sun 12.30pm–4am. This palm-fringed club, bar and restaurant was one of the earliest places in the docks to attract – and then keep – a late-night clientele. The cocktail bar on the esplanade is the latest enticement, while the excellent and reasonable modern take on Portuguese food (grilled fish and meats with pasta or couscous) more than compensates for its position slightly away from the river.

Havana
Armazém 5, Doca de Santo Amaro ☎213 979 893 ⓦwww.havana.com.pt. Daily noon–6am. Cuban-themed bar with wicker chairs and Latin. It also does moderately

▲ DOCA DE SANTO RESTAURANT

▲ SPEAKEASY CLUB

priced salads, toasted sandwiches and the like.

Op Art

Doca de Santo Amaro ☎ 213 956 797 ⓦ www.opartcafe.com. Tues–Sat 1pm–5am. Sat in splendid isolation on the fringes of the Tejo, this small glass pavilion morphs from a minimalist restaurant serving moderately priced grills into a groovy evening bar. After 1pm, the volume pumps up and it turns into more of a dance venue. In summer, you can sprawl on dockside beanbags and gaze over the river.

Queens

Rua Cintura do Porto de Lisboa, Armázem H, Naves A–B ☎ 213 955 870. Tues–Sat 10pm–6am.

Launched as a "high-tech gay disco", this has since successfully attracted a large following of beautiful people of all sexual persuasions. It's a huge, pulsating place – there's an excellent sound system – which can hold up to 2,500 people. Tuesday night is "Ladies' Night" which involves a male strip show; there are visiting DJs on other nights.

Speakeasy

Armazém 115, Cais das Oficinas ☎ 213 957 308. Mon–Sat 10pm–4am. Docklands jazz bar and restaurant presenting a mixture of big and up-and-coming names, usually Tuesday to Thursday after 11pm.

Belém and Ajuda

With its maritime history and attractive riverside location, Belém (pronounced ber-layng) is understandably one of Lisbon's most visited suburbs. It was from Belém that Vasco da Gama set sail for India in 1497; he returned a year later with a cargo of pepper that made enough profit to pay for his voyage sixty times over. The monastery subsequently built here – the Mosteiro dos Jerónimos – stands as a testament to his triumphant discovery of a sea route to the Orient, which initiated the beginning of a Portuguese golden age. Along with the monastery and the landmark Torre de Belém, the suburb boasts a group of small museums, most of them set up under the Salazar regime during the wartime Expo in 1940, though the best of the lot, the Museu do Design, opened in 1999. Just to the north of Belém is Ajuda, famed for its palace and ancient botanical gardens. Higher still lies the extensive parkland of Monsanto, Lisbon's largest green space.

Mosteiro dos Jerónimos

Praça do Império ☎ 213 620 034, ⓦ www.mosteirojeronimos.pt. Daily: June–Sept 10am–6.30pm; Oct–May 10am–5pm; restricted access on Sat mornings and during Mass. Free. A UNESCO World Heritage site, the Mosteiro dos Jerónimos is Portugal's most successful achievement of Manueline architecture. Construction began in 1502, the result of a vow that Dom Manuel had made to the Virgin that he would build a monastery should Vasco da Gama return successfully from his trip to India. The daring of the design is largely the brainchild of Diogo de Boitaca, perhaps the originator of the Manueline style, and João de Castilho, a Spaniard who took charge of construction from around 1517. Castilho designed the main entrance to the church – an arch decorated with a complex hierarchy of figures clustered around Henry the Navigator. Just inside the entrance lie the stone tombs of Vasco da Gama (1468–1523) and the great poet and recorder of the discoveries, Luís de Camões (1527–70).

The breathtaking sense of space inside the church places it

Belém transport

The best way to reach Belém is on **tram** #15 (signed Algés), which runs from Praça da Figueira via Praça do Comércio and Cais do Sodré (roughly 20min); watch out for pickpockets. At Belém, a road train (*comboio turístico*) follows a forty-five-minute circuit (roughly hourly from 10am–7pm, except 1pm; day ticket €3 includes 25 per cent reduction to Museu da Marinha) from the Mosteiro dos Jerónimos to the Museu dos Coches, returning on an uphill route.

▲ MUSEU DE ARQUEOLOGIA

among the greatest triumphs of European Gothic, though Manueline developments add fresh dimensions: there are deliberate tensions between the grand spatial design and the areas of intensely detailed ornamentation. It's difficult to see the six central columns as anything other than palm trunks, growing both into and from the branches of the delicate rib-vaulting.

Vaulted throughout and fantastically embellished, the **cloisters** (€4.50, free Sun 10am–2pm) form one of the most original pieces of architecture in the country. The rounded corner canopies and elegant twisting divisions within each of the arches lend a wave-like, undulating appearance to the whole structure, a conceit extended by the typically Manueline motifs of ropes, anchors and the sea. Round the edges of the cloisters you can still see twelve niches where pilgrims and sailors stopped for confessionals.

Museu de Arqueologia

Praça do Império ☎ 213 620 000 ⓦ www.mnarqueologia-ipmuseus.pt. Tues 2–6pm, Wed–Sun 10am–6pm. €3, free Sun 10am–2pm. Housed in a Neo-Manueline extension to the monastery added in 1850, and dating from 1893, the archeology museum has a small section on Egyptian antiquities dating from 6000 BC, but concentrates on Portuguese archeological finds. It's a sparse collection reprieved by coins and jewellery through the ages, and a few fine Roman mosaics unearthed in the Algarve. Its temporary exhibits can be rewarding.

Museu da Marinha

Praça do Império ☎ 213 620 019. ⓦ www.museumarinha.pt Tues–Sun: April–Sept 10am–6pm; Oct–March 10am–5pm. €3. In the west wing of the monastery extension is an absorbing maritime museum, packed not only with models of ships, naval uniforms and artefacts from Portugal's oriental trade and colonies, but also with

▲ FISHING BOAT, MUSEU DA MARINHA

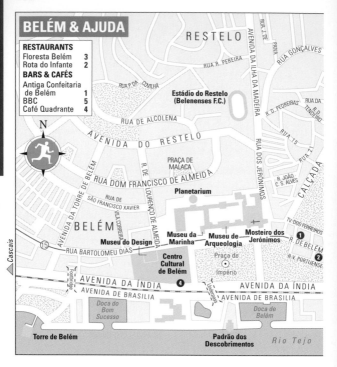

BELÉM & AJUDA

RESTAURANTS
Floresta Belém — 3
Rota do Infante — 2
BARS & CAFÉS
Antiga Confeitaria
de Belém — 1
BBC — 5
Café Quadrante — 4

real vessels – among them fishing boats and sumptuous state barges, early seaplanes and some ancient fire engines.

Praça do Império

The formal gardens and walkways that make up Praça do Império are laid out over Belém's former beach, and accommodate hundreds of daily visitors to Belém. It's especially busy on Saturday mornings, when there seems to be an endless procession of flamboyant weddings at the monastery, whose photo-calls invariably spill out into the square. The attractive seventeenth-century buildings along Rua Vieira Portuense are now mostly restaurants with

outdoor seating; as a rule, the further east you head, the better value and less touristy they become.

Centro Cultural de Belém

Praça do Império ☎ 213 612 400, ⓦ www.ccb.pt. The stylish, modern, pink marble Centro Cultural de Belém was built to host Lisbon's 1992 presidency of the European Union. It's now one of the city's main cultural centres, containing a design museum and hosting regular photography and art exhibitions, as well as concerts and shows. There are also plans for the centre to display many of the stunning works of modern art collected by the Berardo Foundation (see p.145).

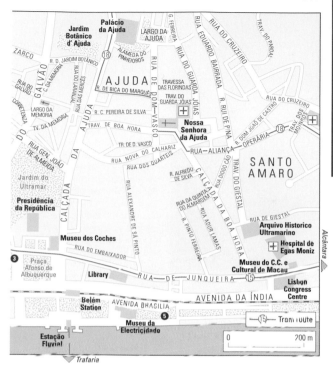

Trafaria

Museu do Design

Praça do Império ☎ 213 612 400. Daily 11am–8pm (last entry at 7.15pm). €3.50. The Museu do Design (Design Museum) is the first in the city dedicated to contemporary household design and is considered one of the most important in Europe. The collection contains over six hundred design classics, embracing furniture, glass and jewellery from 1937 to the present day and is so big that exhibits are rotated, though the most important items usually remain on display.

These are shown chronologically in three sections entitled "Luxo", "Pop" and "Cool". "Luxo" contains one-off luxury and later industrially produced designs from the 1930s to the 1950s, including classic fibreglass chairs by Charles and Ray Eames, and

▼ CENTRO CULTURAL DE BELÉM

▲ PADRÃO DOS DESCOBRIMENTOS

Marshmallow and Coconut chairs by the American George Nelson. "Pop" features fun designs from the 1960s and 1970s, including bean-bags, kitsch moulded plastic furniture and an amazingly elaborate Joe Colombo Mino Kitchen, designed in 1963. "Cool" shows off work from the 1980s and 1990s, including the Memphis Group's *Tawaraya* bed, Phillipe Starck's chair and the creations of established Portuguese designers such as Tomás Tavira and Álvaro Siza Vieria.

Padrão dos Descobrimentos

Avenida de Brasília, reached via an underpass beneath the Avenida da Índia and railway line ☎213 016 228. Tues–Sun: June–Sept 9am–6.30pm; Nov–May 9am–5pm. €2. The Padrão dos Descobrimentos (Monument to the Discoveries) is a 54-metre high, caravel-shaped slab of concrete erected in 1960 to commemorate the five-hundredth anniversary of the death of Henry the

Navigator. An impressively large and detailed statue of Henry appears at the head of a line of statues that feature Luís de Camões and other Portuguese heroes. Within the monument is a small exhibition space, with interesting temporary exhibits on the city's history – the entrance fee also includes a ride in the lift to the top for some fine views of the Tejo and the Torre de Belém. Just in front of the monument, tourists pose on the marble pavement decorated with a map of the world charting the routes taken by the great Portuguese explorers of the fifteenth to seventeenth centuries.

Torre de Belém

☎213 620 034. Tues–Sun: June–Sept 10am–6.30pm; Oct–May 10am–5pm. €3. The Torre de Belém, 500m west of the monastery, was built over the last five years of Dom Manuel's reign (1515–20) to defend the mouth of the Tejo – before an earthquake shifted the river's course in 1777, the tower stood near the middle of the waters. The tower is the country's only example of a building started and completed during the Manueline era (the rest having been adaptations of earlier structures or completed in later years) and has become the favoured symbol used to promote Lisbon by the Portuguese Tourist Board.

Its Moorish influence is clear in the delicately arched windows and balconies. Prominent also in the decoration are two great icons of the age: Manuel's personal badge of an armillary sphere (representing the globe); and the cross of the military Order of Christ, once the Templars, who took a major role in all the

Portuguese conquests. Clamber up the steep internal stairs via a series of bare rooms for great views from the top. When inside, it is also easy to imagine what it was like in the nineteenth century when it was used as a prison, notoriously by Dom Miguel (1828–34), who kept political enemies in the waterlogged dungeons.

Jardim do Ultramar

Entrance on Calçada do Galvão. Daily 10am–5pm. €1.50. The leafy Jardim do Ultramar is an oasis of hothouses, ponds and towering palms, a lovely place for a shady walk. In the southeastern corner of the garden lies the Portuguese President's official residence, the pink Presidência da República.

Estádio do Restelo

Avenida do Restelo ☎ 213 010 461, ⊛ www.cfbelenenses.pt. The attractively sited Estádio do Restelo is home to Belenenses soccer club, Lisbon's third team. Belenenses has won just one league title, back in 1946, but the stadium offers such picturesque views over the river that the soccer action is almost insignificant. Top teams (Porto, Benfica and the like) frequently visit.

Museu dos Coches

Praça Afonso de Albuquerque ☎ 213 610 850. ⊛ www.museudoscoches-ipmuseus.pt. Tues–Sun 10am–6pm, free Sun 10am–2pm. €3. Once the home of the royal riding school, the Museu dos Coches (coach museum) was opened in 1905 on the initiative of the queen, Dona Amélia, and contains one of the largest collections of carriages and saddlery in the world. Baroque, heavily gilded and sometimes beautifully painted, the coaches date from the sixteenth to nineteenth centuries. From the same period are sedan chairs, children's buggies and a very rare sixteenth-century coach designed for King Felipe I (Spain's King Philip II).

Museu da Electricidade

Avenida de Brasília ☎ 213 425 401. Tues–Fri & Sun 10am–12.30pm & 2–5.30pm, Sat 10am–12.30pm & 2–8pm. €2. The extraordinary redbrick Museu da Electricidade (Electricity Museum) is housed in an early twentieth-century electricity generating station. The highlights include a series of enormous generators, steam turbines and winches – resembling a set from the science-fiction film *Brazil*. It's a highly atmospheric place and hosts occasional art and

▼ TORRE DE BELÉM

technology exhibitions. From in front of the museum, it is possible to walk the 1.5km along the lawned riverside all the way to the Doca de Santo Amaro one way, or the 1km to central Belém the other way.

Palácio da Ajuda

Largo da Ajuda ☎213 637 095. Tram #18 from Praça do Comércio or bus #14 from Belém. One-hour tours every 30min Mon, Tues & Thurs–Sun 10am–4.30pm. €4, free Sun 10am–2pm.
This massive nineteenth-century palace sits on a hillside above Belém. Construction began in 1802, but was left incomplete when João VI and the royal family fled to Brazil to escape Napoleon's invading army in 1807. The original plans were therefore never fulfilled, though the completed section was used as a royal residence after João returned from exile in 1821. The surviving decor was commissioned by the crashingly tasteless nineteenth-century royals, Dona Maria II (João's granddaughter) and Dom Ferdinand and is all over-the-top aristocratic clutter. The highly ornate banqueting hall, however, is impressive, full of crystal chandeliers, as is the lift, decked out with mahogany and mirrors. The palace is occasionally used for classical music concerts.

Jardim Botânico d'Ajuda

Opposite the palace. Entrance on Calçada da Ajuda. Mon, Tues & Thurs–Sun 9am–dusk. €1.75. This is one of the city's oldest and most interesting botanical gardens. Commissioned by the Marquês de Pombal and laid out in 1768, it was owned by the royal family until the birth of the Republic in 1910, then substantially restored in the 1990s. The garden is divided into eight parts planted with plant species from around the world, all arranged around a system of terraces, statues and fountains – a fine example of formal Portuguese gardening.

Parque Florestal de Monsanto

Bus #43. The extensive, wooded hillside Parque Florestal de Monsanto – home to the city's main campsite – is known as "'Lisbon's lungs" but its main attraction was for prostitutes and their clients until the Mayor of Lisbon bought a house nearby in 2003. Suddenly the park has been given a new lease of life: hookers have been replaced by horse-and-trap rides to its splendid viewpoints, while at weekends in summer the whole area is completely traffic-free. Summer pop concerts are laid on most weekends, usually free of charge.

Cafés and bars

Antiga Confeitaria de Belém

Rua de Belém 90. Daily 8am–11pm.
No visit to Belém is complete without a coffee and hot *pastel de nata* (custard-cream tart) liberally sprinkled with *canela* (cinnamon) in this cavernous, tiled pastry shop and café, which has been serving them up since 1837. The place positively heaves, especially at weekends, but there's usually space to sit down in its warren of rooms.

BBC

Avenida Brasília, Pavilhão Poente. Daily 12.30pm–midnight, bar until 3.30am.
Those at Bush House would probably approve of the Belém Bar Café borrowing their initials

– this swish place exudes class. A glass roof throws light onto a huge central bar area cooled by spinning fans. Enjoy river views as you tuck into mains of grilled meats, fish and pasta (€12–19), while the bar area has comfy sofas, a roof terrace and pumping music. Minimum consumption is around €15.

Café Quadrante

Centro Cultural de Belém. Mon–Fri 10am–8pm, Sat & Sun 10am–9pm. Part of the Belém Cultural Centre, offering good-value self-service food from two counters. The best place to enjoy its coffee and snacks is on the outdoor terrace by the roof gardens, overlooking the bridge, river and Monument to the Discoveries. It's so popular with students that they are forbidden from studying here at mealtimes.

Restaurants

Floresta Belém

Praça Afonso de Albuquerque 1. Mon–Sat 9am–4pm & 6.30pm–midnight, Sun 9am–4pm. On the corner with Rua Vieira Portuense, this

▲ HOUSES AND RESTAURANTS ON RUA VIERA PORTUENSE

attracts a largely Portuguese clientele, especially for lunch at the weekend. Great salads, grills and fresh fish from around €6, served inside or on a sunny outdoor terrace.

Rota do Infante

Rua Vieira Portuense 10–14 ☎213 646 787. Tues–Sun noon–3pm & 7.30–11pm. One of the many places in this pretty row of buildings facing the greenery of Praça do Império. Decently priced fish and meat with outdoor seats under fragrant orange trees.

Avenida da Liberdade and around

The grand, palm-lined Avenida da Liberdade is still much as Fernando Pessoa described it: "the finest artery in Lisbon... full of trees ...small gardens, ponds, fountains, cascades and statues". The 1.3-kilometre-long avenue, together with its side streets, was once home to statesmen and public figures, including António Medeiros, an art collector whose works are now displayed in a fine town-house museum. On the western side of the avenue it's a short walk to the historic Praça das Amoreiras, the finishing point of the massive Aqueduto das Águas Livres. Here you'll find the Fundação Arpad Siznes-Viera da Silva, a collection of works by two artists heavily influenced by Lisbon.

Avenida da Liberdade

Avenida da Liberdade was laid out in 1882 and is the city's main central avenue, with appealing outdoor cafés under the shade of trees that help cushion the roar of the passing traffic. Some of the avenue's original nineteenth-century mansions remain, though most have been replaced by modern buildings. The upper end of the avenue houses many of the city's designer shops and airline offices and ends in a swirl of traffic at the landmark roundabout of Praça Marquês de Pombal, also known as Rotunda.

Parque Mayer

Opened in 1922 as an "entertainment precinct" when theatres were all the rage, the **Parque Mayer** is still one of the capital's main destinations for theatregoers. It is about to be given a makeover by Frank Gehry, architect of the Guggenheim in Bilbao. This may lead to the controversial demolishing of the listed Teatro Capitólio – not the most handsome of theatres, but its concrete angular form is the country's first great Modernist structure.

Elevador do Lavra

Mon–Sat 7am–9pm, Sun 9am–9pm. €1.20. Starting at the little

▼ ELEVADOR DO LAVRA

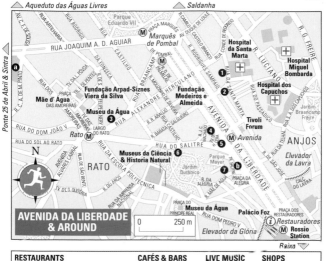

RESTAURANTS		CAFÉS & BARS	LIVE MUSIC	SHOPS
O Cantinho do Rato **3**	Ribadouro **5**	Rela Ipanema **4**	Hot Clube	Amoreiras **a**
Marisqueira	Tibetanos **6**	Pastelaria Santa	de Portugal **7**	Casa do Turista **b**
Santa Marta **1**		Marta **2**		

square of Largo da Anunciada, the Elevador do Lavra funicular opened in 1882 and is Lisbon's least tourist-frequented *elevador*. Take a ride to the top of the precipitous slope, where a short walk down Travessa do Torel on the left takes you to **Jardim do Torel**, a tiny park offering exhilarating views over Lisbon.

Fundação Medeiros e Almeida

Rua Rosa Araújo 41 ☎ 213 547 892. Mon–Sat 1–5.30pm. €5. The Fundação Medeiros e Almeida was the home of the industrialist, philanthropist and art collector António Medeiros until his death in 1986. Today it serves as a showcase for his priceless series of artefacts. His collection of 225 Chinese porcelain items (some 2000 years old), sixteenth- to nineteenth-century watches, and English and Portuguese

silverware are considered the most valuable in the world. Other highlights include glorious eighteenth-century azulejos in the Sala do Lago, a room complete with large water fountains; and a rare seventeenth-century clock, made for Queen Catherine of Bragança and mentioned by Samuel Pepys in his diary.

Fundação Arpad Siznes-Viera da Silva

Praça das Amoreiras 58 ☎ 213 880 044. Mon & Wed–Sat noon–8pm, Sun 10am–6pm. €2.50. Set in a former eighteenth-century silk factory, the Fundação Arpad Siznes-Viera da Silva is a small but highly appealing gallery dedicated to the works of two painters and the artists who have been influenced by them. Arpad Siznes (1897–1985) was a Hungarian-born artist and friend of Henri Matisse and

Pierre Bonnard, amongst others. In 1928, while working as a caricaturist in Paris, he met the Portuguese artist Maria Helena Viera da Silva (1908–92), whose work was influenced by the surrealism of Joan Miró and Max Ernst, both of whom she was good friends with. Siznes and Viera da Silva married in 1930 and, in 1936, both exhibited in Lisbon, where they briefly lived, before eventually settling in France. The foundation shows the development of the artists' works, with Viera da Silva's more abstract, subdued paintings contrasting with flamboyant Siznes, some of whose paintings show the clear influence of Miró.

Praça das Amoreiras

One of Lisbon's most tranquil squares, Praça das Amoreiras – complete with a kiosk café (closed Sat) and kids' play area – is dominated on its western side by the final section of the **Aqueduto das Águas Livres**

(Free Waters Aqueduct), with a chapel wedged into its arches. The aqueduct was opened in 1748, bringing a reliable source of safe drinking water.

On the south side of Praça das Amoreiras, the **Mãe d'Água** cistern (☎218 135 522; Mon–Sat 10am–6pm; €2.50) marks the end of the line for the aqueduct. Built between 1746 and 1834, the castellated stone building contains a resevoir where the water was stored and distributed round the city. The structure nowadays hosts occasional temporary art exhibitions. Head to the back where there are stairs leading on to the roof for great views over the city.

Aqueduto das Águas Livres

Entrance on Calçada da Quintinha 6 ☎218 100 215. March–Oct daily 10am–6pm. €2.50. Bus #58. Accessed off a quiet residential street through a small park in Campolide, 1km north of Praça das Amoreiras, you can walk right across the central section of Lisbon's towering aqueduct (see left), a dizzy hike not recommended to vertigo sufferers. The entire structure stretches some 60km, mostly underground, though the walkable section is around 1.5km. The structure stood firm during the 1755 earthquake, though it later gained a more notorious reputation thanks to one Diogo Alves, a nineteenth-century serial killer who threw his victims off the top – a seventy-metre drop.

▼ PRAÇA DAS AMOREIRAS AQUEDUCT ARCHES

▲ PASTELARIA ANUNCIADA

Shops

Amoreiras

Entrance on Avenida Engenheiro Duarte Pacheco. Daily 10am–midnight. Bus #11 or #58. Amoreiras, Lisbon's eye-catching, post-modern commercial centre, is visible on the city skyline from almost any approach. Built in 1985 and designed by adventurous Portuguese architect Tomás Taveira, it is a wild fantasy of pink and blue towers sheltering ten cinemas, sixty cafés and restaurants, 250 shops and a hotel. Most stores are open from around 10pm until midnight seven days a week; Sunday sees the heaviest human traffic, with entire families descending for an afternoon out.

Casa do Turista

Avda da Liberdade 159. Crammed with T-shirts and arts, crafts and ceramics from Portugal's various regions, this tourist gift shop is not too pricey and though some stuff is tacky there's plenty of gift potential including some fine toy trams.

Cafés and bars

Bela Ipanema

Avda da Liberdade 169. A bustling café/bar/restaurant by the São Jorge cinema where a steady stream of locals pop in for pastries, light lunches, beers and coffees at the bar or in its small dining area that serves very good-value food; outdoor tables face the avenue.

Pastelaria Santa Marta

Rua Rodrigues Sampaio 52. Unglamorous but popular local haunt with a superb array of cakes and snacks. A good spot for inexpensive lunches. Pay at the till on exit.

Restaurants

O Cantinho do Rato

Mercado do Rato, entrance off Rua Alexandre Herculano 64 ☎213 883 160. Mon–Sat noon–3pm.

▼ BELA IPANEMA

Tucked away up a side alley next to Rato's fruit, fish and clothes market and open for lunches only. Geared for market workers; grills are large, satisfying and very good value, from around €5.

Marisqueira Santa Marta

Trav. do Enviato de Inglaterra 1 (off Rua de Santa Marta) ☎213 525 638. Daily 9am–midnight. Attractive and spacious *marisqueira* with bubbling tanks of crabs in one corner. Service is very attentive and meals end with a complimentary port, after which you don't usually care that the bill is slightly above average.

Ribadouro

Avda da Liberdade 155 ☎213 549 411. Daily noon–1am. The *avenida*'s best *cervejaria*, serving superb mixed grills (around €13), speciality prawns with garlic (around €15) and pricier shellfish (but no fish). If you don't fancy a full meal, take a seat at the bar and order a beer with a plate of prawns. It's best to book for the restaurant, especially at weekends.

Tibetanos

Rua do Salitre 117 ☎213 142 038. Mon–Fri noon–2pm & 7.30–9.30pm. Run by a Buddhist centre, this stripped-pine restaurant has

▲ KIOSK CAFÉ, AVENIDA DA LIBERDADE

superb and unusual moderately priced veggie food, including crepes, curries, quiches and desserts such as papaya pie.

Live music

Hot Clube de Portugal

Praça da Alegria 39 ☎213 467 369 ⓦwww.hcp.pt. Tues–Sat 10pm–2am. The city's best jazz venue, a tiny basement club hosting local and visiting artists. It's appropriately named as it can get very steamy in summer, but there's a tiny courtyard to escape to if things get too hot.

Parque Eduardo VII and the Gulbenkian

On a steep slope to the north of the centre, Parque Eduardo VII is the city's principal park, best known for its views and enormous *estufas*, or hothouses. Northwest of the park, everyone should make the effort to visit the Fundação Calouste Gulbenkian, Portugal's premier cultural centre. This combines one of Europe's richest art collections, on display in the Museu Gulbenkian, whilst Portuguese contemporary art is shown in the nearby Centro de Arte Moderna. Art-lovers have a further attraction to the east in the Saldanha district, where you can view the historic paintings and objects in the Casa Museu Dr Anastácio Gonçalves.

Parque Eduardo VII

The steep, formally laid-out Parque Eduardo VII was named to honour Britain's King Edward VII when he visited the city in 1903. Its main building is the ornately tiled Pavilhão dos Desportos (Sports Pavilion), which doubles as a venue for occasional concerts and cultural events. North of here, two concrete poles and a modern memorial to the earthquake mark a viewing platform with commanding views over Lisbon. In summer, the platform is usually capped by a ferris wheel. Another highlight if you have children is the superb Parque Infantil (open daily; free), a play area built round a mock galleon.

Two huge, rambling **estufas** (daily: Estufa Fria April–Sept 9am–6pm; Oct–March 9am–5pm; Estufa Quente closes 30min earlier; €1.50) lie close by, both filled with tropical plants, pools and endless varieties of palms and cacti. Of the two, the Estufa Quente (the hothouse) has the more exotic plants; the Estufa Fria (the coldhouse) hosts concerts and exhibitions.

Finally, the northern reaches of the park contain an appealing grassy hillock complete with its own olive grove and a shallow lake which kids splash about in during the heat of the day.

Fundação Calouste Gulbenkian

☎ 217 823 000, ⊛ www.gulbenkian. org. Set in extensive leafy

▼ GULBENKIAN GARDENS

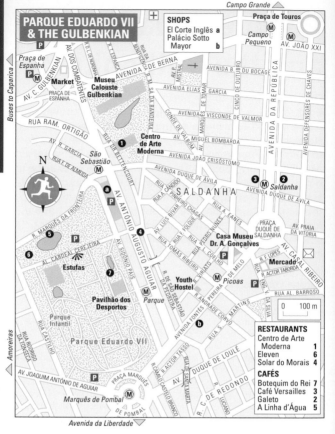

Campo Grande

PARQUE EDUARDO VII & THE GULBENKIAN

SHOPS
El Corte Inglês **a**
Palácio Sotto
Mayor **b**

Praça de Touros

Campo Pequeno

AV. JOÃO XXI

Buses to Caparica

Praça de Espanha

Market

Museu Calouste Gulbenkian

Centro de Arte Moderna ❶

São Sebastião

SALDANHA

Saldanha ❷ ❸

Casa Museu Dr. A. Gonçalves

Mercado ❹

Youth Hostel

Picoas ❹

Estufas

Pavilhão dos Desportos

Parque

Parque Infantil

Parque Eduardo VII

Amoreiras

Marquês de Pombal

Avenida da Liberdade

0   100 m

RESTAURANTS
Centro de Arte
  Moderna   1
Eleven   6
Solar do Morais   4

CAFÉS
Botequim do Rei   7
Café Versailles   3
Galeto   5
A Linha d'Água   5

grounds, the Fundação Calouste Gulbenkian was set up by the Armenian oil magnate Calouste Gulbenkian (1869–1955), whose legendary art-market coups included the acquisition of works from the Hermitage in St Petersburg. Today the Gulbenkian Foundation has a multi-million dollar budget sufficient to finance work in all spheres of Portuguese cultural life. In this low-rise 1960s complex alone, it runs an orchestra, three concert halls and an attractive open-air amphitheatre.

Museu Calouste Gulbenkian

Entrance on Avenida de Berna ☎217 823 000, ⊛www.gulbenkian.pt. Tues–Sun 10am–5.45pm. €3, free Sun, combined ticket with Centro de Arte Moderna €5. The Museu Calouste Gulbenkian covers virtually every phase of Eastern and Western art from their beginnings to the modern era. The small Egyptian room displays art from the Old Kingdom (circa 2700 BC) up to the Roman period. Fine Roman statues, silver and glass, and gold jewellery from ancient Greece follow. The Islamic arts are magnificently represented by a variety of ornamental texts, opulently woven carpets, glassware and Turkish tiles. There is also porcelain from China, and beautiful Japanese prints and lacquer-work.

European art includes work from all the major schools. From fifteenth-century Flanders, there is a pair of panels by Rogier van der Weyden. The seventeenth-century collection yields Peter Paul Rubens' graphic *The Love of the Centaurs* (1635) and Rembrandt's *Figure of an Old Man*. Featured eighteenth-century works include those by Jean-Honoré Fragonard, Thomas Gainsborough – in particular the stunning *Portrait of Mrs Lowndes-Stone* – and Francesco Guardi. The big names of nineteenth- to twentieth-century France – Edouard Manet, Claude Monet, Edgar Degas, Millet and Auguste Renoir – are all represented, along with Turner's vivid *Wreck of a Transport Ship* (1810). Elsewhere you'll find ceramics from Spain and Italy, Sèvres porcelain and furniture from the reigns of Louis XV and Louis XVI, and assorted Italian tapestries and textiles. The last room features an amazing Art Nouveau collection of 169 pieces of fantasy jewellery by René Lalique; the highlight is the fantastical *Peitoral-libélula* (*Dragonfly breastpiece*) brooch, half-woman, half-dragonfly, decorated with enamel work, gold, diamonds and moonstones.

Centro de Arte Moderna José Azeredo Perdigão

Main entrance on Rua Dr Nicolau de Bettencourt ☎217 823 000, ⓦwww .gulbenkian.org. Tues–Sun 10am–5.45pm. €3, free Sun, combined ticket with Museu Calouste Gulbenkian €5. To reach the Centro de Arte Moderna from the Museu Calouste Gulbenkian you can walk through the gardens, which are enlivened by some specially commissioned sculptures (including a Henry Moore).

The centre embraces pop art, installations and sculptures – some witty, some baffling, but all thought-provoking. Most of the big names on the twentieth-century Portuguese scene feature, including black-and-white panels by Almada Negreiros (1873–1970), the founder of *modernismo* (his self-portrait is set in the café *A Brasileira*, see p.87), the bright Futurist colours of Amadeu de Sousa Cardoso, and Paula Rego

PLACES Parque Eduardo VII and the Gulbenkian

▲ VIEW FROM TOP OF PARQUE EDUARDO VII

(one of Portugal's leading contemporary artists, now resident in England), whose *Mãe* (1997) is outstanding. There are subtle abstracts and sculptures by American expressionist Arshile Gorky, and powerful photos by Fernando Lemos (1926). British artists also feature; most striking are the prostrate figure of a man, *Close II,* by Anthony Gormley and Bill Woodrow's wooden *War-head* sculpture.

Casa Museu Dr Anastácio Gonçalves

Avda 5 de Outubro 8. Entrance on Rua Pinheiro Chagas. ☏ 213 540 823, ⓦ www.cmag-ipmuseus.pt. Tues 2–6pm, Wed–Sun 10am–6pm. €2. The appealing Neo-Romantic building with Art Nouveau touches – including a beautiful stained-glass window – was originally built for the painter José Malhoa in 1904, but now holds the exquisite private collection of ophthalmologist Dr Anastácio Gonçalves, who bought the house in the 1930s. Highlights include paintings by Portuguese landscape artist João Vaz and by Malhoa himself, who specialized in historical paintings

▲ CASA MUSEU DR ANASTÁCIO GONÇALVES

– his *Dream of Infante Henriques* is a typical example. On the top floor you'll find Chinese porcelain from the sixteenth-century Ming dynasty, along with furniture from England, France, Holland and Spain dating from the seventeenth century. The downstairs rooms also host temporary exhibits, from historical costume to contemporary art.

Shops

El Corte Inglês

Avda António Augusto de Aguiar. Closed Sun. Cinema info on ☏ 707 232 221. A giant Spanish department store spread over nine floors, two of which are underground. The basement specializes in gourmet food, with various delis, bakers and a supermarket (closed Sun afternoon), while the upper floors offer a range of stylish goods, including clothes, sports gear, books, CDs and toys. The top floor packs in cafés and restaurants with an outdoor terrace. There's also a fourteen-screen cinema in the basement.

Palácio Sotto Mayor

Avda Fontes Pereira de Melo 16. Most shops daily 10am–9pm. A former banker's mansion hollowed out into an ornately decorated shopping emporium and gallery space. Small boutiques showcase designer jewellery and clothing.

Cafés and bars

Botequim do Rei

Esplanade da Parque Eduardo VII. Tues–Sun 10am–9pm. The fish and meat dishes on offer here are fairly average but the outdoor seating, right in the park by a small lake, is particularly tranquil, making this a good place to head for lunch or a drink. Take care here, though, after dark.

▲ ESTUFA HOUSE

Café Versailles

Avda da República 15a. Daily 7.30am–10pm. Traditional café full of bustling waiters circling the starched tablecloths. It's busiest at around 4pm, when Lisbon's elderly dames gather for a chat beneath the chandeliers.

Galeto

Avda da República 14 ☎213 560 269. Daily 7am–4am. Late-opening café-bar with striking 1950s' decor: dark, metal-studded walls and padded bar seats. There's a great range of snacks, pastries, beers and coffees.

A Linha d'Água

Parque Eduardo VII Daily 10.30am–9pm. Facing a small lake, this glass-fronted café is at the northern end of the park. It's not a bad spot to sip a coffee or beer, and decent buffet lunches are served too.

Restaurants

Centro de Arte Moderna

Rua Dr Bettencourt, Fundação Calouste Gulbenkian. Tues–Sun 10am–5.45pm. Join the lunchtime queues at the museum restaurant for bargain hot and cold dishes. There's an excellent choice of salads for vegetarians. Similar fare is offered in the basement of the Gulbenkian museum, with outdoor seats facing the gardens.

Eleven

Rua Marquês da Fronteira ☎213 862 211 ⓦ www.restauranteleven.com.

Tues–Sat 12.30pm–11pm. At the top of Parque Eduardo VII, this Michelin-starred restaurant hits the heights both literally and metaphorically. The interior is both intimate and bright with wonderful city views. Quality here is expensive but not outrageous, with set menus from around €70. Dishes feature Azorean tuna with sesame, ox consommé with ginger and lobster ravioli or wasabi risotto with prawn crunch, and there's a fine wine list.

Solar do Morais

Rua Augusto dos Santos 3. Mon–Fri & Sun 9.30am–10.30pm. Very much a locals' joint, despite its position between the tourist draws of Parque Eduardo VII and the Gulbenkian. The cool, arched interior has cabinets of fresh food, bottles lining the walls and a large ham on the bar. Good-value trout and salmon dishes are always worth ordering, and there's a small outdoor terrace.

▲ ELEVEN

Northern Lisbon

Aside from using the bus station, few visitors explore the bustling modern suburbs north of the Gulbenkian. The one must-see sight is the Palácio dos Marquêses de Fronteira, famed for its collection of azulejos. Two modern soccer stadiums – home to European giants Sporting Lisbon and Benfica – will also feature on many itineraries. The latter has the bonus of Iberia's largest shopping complex and funfair on its doorstep. To the south is the city's main bullring at Campo Pequeno, while east lies Parque Bela Vista, home to the Rock in Rio festival.

Praça de Touros

Campo Pequeno ☏ 217 998 453. Built in 1892, the Praça de Touros do Campo Pequeno is an impressive Moorish-style bullring seating nine thousand spectators. The Portuguese *tourada* (bullfight) is neither as commonplace nor as famous as its Spanish counterpart, but as a spectacle it's marginally preferable, as here the bull isn't killed in the ring, but instead is wrestled to the ground in a genuinely elegant, colourful and skilled display. During the fight, however, the bull is usually injured and it is always slaughtered later in any case. Performances start at 10pm on Thursday evenings from Easter to September. The bullring also hosts visiting circuses and occasional events, while beneath is an underground shopping and cinema complex.

Culturgest

Avenida João XXI 63 ☏ 217 905 155, ⓦ www.dgd.pt. The 1980s monolith Culturgest arts complex runs regular art exhibitions and film seasons and hosts performances of classical music.

Estádio José Alvalade

Rua Professor da Fonseca ☏ 217 516 000, ⓦ www.sporting.pt. Tickets for games (from €10) are available from booths at the ground or online. This state-of-the-art stadium was purpose-built as one of Lisbon's two venues for the 2004 European Championships, with a capacity of 54,000. It is home to Sporting Clube de Portugal – usually known as Sporting Lisbon, one of Portugal's three big soccer clubs, which celebrated its centenary in 2006. Sporting have established themselves as Lisbon's most successful team of the new millennium, eclipsing closest rivals Benfica. Stadium visits can be arranged on request.

Parque Bela Vista

Opened in 2000, this park consists of 200,000 square metres of sloping lawns and trees. Though pleasant enough, the park is only really worth visiting for May's biannual rock festival, Rock in Rio (ⓦ www. rockinrio-lisboa.sapo.pt), one of the world's biggest. Over five days, up to half a million people visit for live music, family entertainment and even an artificial ski slope. Past

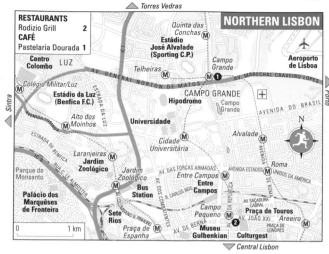

performers have featured stars
from various decades including
The Red Hot Chili Peppers,
Guns 'N Roses, Sting, Shakira
and Santana.

Jardim Zoológico

Estrada de Benfica ☏ 217 232 910,
ⓦ www.zoolisboa.pt. Daily: April–Sept
10am–8pm; Oct–March 10am–6pm.
€12, children under 12 €9.
Lisbon's zoo, the Jardim
Zoológico, was opened in 1884
and makes for an enjoyable
afternoon's ramble. Indeed
there's a substantial café-lined
park area which you can visit
for free and see monkeys,
crocodiles and parrots. Once
inside the zoo proper, a small
cable car (daily from 11am until
30min before closing; included
in the price) transports you over
many of the animals and there's
a well-stocked reptile house
(11am–7.30pm) as further
diversion. Just by its main gates
lies the Animax amusement
park (daily 11am–8pm), where
kids can load up a card for rides
and games to relieve their
parents of further euros.

Palácio dos Marquêses de Fronteira

Largo de São Domingos de Benfica 1
☏ 217 782 023. Tours Mon–Sat: June–
Sept at 10.30am, 11am, 11.30am &
noon; Oct–May at 11am & noon. €5
weekdays, €7.50 weekends. Gardens
only €3 weekdays, €2.50 weekends.
Reservations advised. Bus #46 passes
nearby, or it's a 20min walk from the
zoo. You don't need to be a
dyed-in-the-wool palace
enthusiast to enjoy a visit to the
Palácio dos Marquêses de
Fronteira, a seventeenth-century
former hunting lodge on the
northeastern fringes of the
Parque de Monsanto. Built in
1670 for the first Marquês de
Fronteira, João de Mascarenhas,
and still inhabited by
descendants of the same family,
the palace has been partly open
to the public since 1989. The
formal gardens are particularly
fine, complete with ornate
topiary, statues and fountains,
but it's the interior that
impresses the most, notably the
stunning azulejos dating back to
the seventeenth century. Some
of the rooms are completely

lined with them, including the Sala das Batalhas (Battle Room), whose tiles depict vivid scenes from the Restoration Wars with Spain. Guided tours of the interior last about an hour, after which you're free to wander in the gardens.

Estádio da Luz

Avenida General Norton de Matos ☎217 219 500, ⓦwww.slbenfica.pt. Tickets for games (€22–32) are available from booths at the ground or online. The Estádio da Luz is one of Europe's most famous stadiums – the English team Sunderland even stole its name ("Stadium of Light"), which actually derives from the name of the suburb Luz rather than its illuminations. Home to Benfica (officially called Sport Lisboa e Benfica) the stadium was rebuilt

as the main venue for the Euro 2004 football championships, with a capacity of seventy thousand. Along with Porto, Benfica has historically dominated the Portuguese championship: it was European champion in 1961–62, and runner-up in 1968, 1988 and 1990. However, recent years have been difficult, with the club rocked by financial irregularities, though it did win the championship in 2005.

Shops

Centro Colombo

Avenida Lusíada. Cinema info on ☎217 113 200. Iberia's largest shopping centre, Centro Colombo, is almost a town in its own right, with over 400 shops, 65 restaurants and 11 cinema screens. Major stores include FNAC, C&A, Zara, Habitat and Toys "R" Us, while the top floor has the usual fast-food outlets along with a sit-down dining area in the jungle-themed "Cidade Perdida" (Lost City). There is also a "Fun Centre" (daily: noon–midnight) which claims to be Europe's largest covered amusement park, complete with rides, roundabouts, bumper cars, ten-pin bowling and even a roller-coaster that whizzes overhead.

▲ SPORTING LISBON STADIUM

An additional outdoor area features mini-bungee jumps, a go-kart track and toy car and boat rides.

Cafés

Pastelaria Dourada

Rua Cipriano Dourado. Daily 6.30am–10pm. Bustling café-bar right by Sporting Lisbon's ground. Serves bargain beers, coffee, pizzas or snacks (pay at the till before getting your order from the bar).

Restaurants

Rodizio Grill

Campo Pequeno 79 ☎ 217 800 453. Daily noon–4pm & 7.30pm–midnight. Right opposite the bullring, this huge, industrial place appropriately specializes in Brazilian *rodizio* – various types of barbecued meats – with a

▲ CENTRO COLOMBO

salad bar as a token healthy option. It's good value if you have a big appetite as, for €20, you can top your plate up as often as you like.

Parque das Nações

The Parque das Nações (Park of Nations) is the name
given to the former site of Expo 98, purpose-built to
coincide with the 500th anniversary of Vasco da Gama's
arrival in India. Its flat, traffic-free walkways lined with
fountains and futuristic buildings are in complete
contrast to the narrow, precipitous streets of old Lisbon,
and it is a very popular destination for Lisboetas,
especially during summer weekends. The main highlight
is the Oceanário de Lisboa, Europe's second-largest
oceanarium. Other attractions include water gardens, a
cable car, and two of Lisbon's largest concert venues. It
is also impossible to miss the astonishing seventeen-
kilometre-long Vasco da Gama bridge over the Tejo,
which dominates the river at this point.

Olivais dock and the Pavilhão Atlântico

The central focus of the
Parque das Nações is the
Olivais dock, overlooked by
pixie-hatted twin towers, and
where boats pull in on Tejo
cruises (see p184). The dock's
Nautical Centre (☎218 918
532) offers canoeing, sailing
and windsurfing lessons. The
main building facing the dock
is the Pavilhão de Portugal
(Portugal Pavilion), a multipurpose arena designed by
Álvaro Siza Vieira, architect
of the reconstructed Chiado

▲ OLIVAIS DOCK

Visiting the park

Oriente metro station exits in the bowels of the Estação do Oriente, a cavernous
glass and concrete station designed by Spanish architect Santiago Calatrava.

The Posto de Informação (information desk; daily 10am–8pm, until 7pm from
Oct–April; ☎218 919 333, ⊛www.parquedasnacoes.pt) has details of the day's
events. If you want to visit everything, it is worth buying a Cartão do Parque
(€16.50, or €8.50 for children under 12) from the desk. This allows free access
to the main sights and discounts at other attractions.

It's easy to walk round the park, or there's a toy train, which trundles anti-
clockwise around the main sights (hourly 10am–7pm; until 5pm from Oct–April;
€2.50). You can also hire bikes from Tejo Bike behind the information desk for €4
an hour.

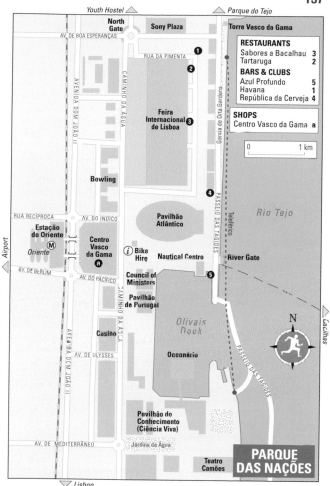

Youth Hostel △   △ Parque do Tejo

North Gate
Sony Plaza   Torre Vasco da Gama
AV. DE BOA ESPERANÇAS

RUA DA PIMENTA   **RESTAURANTS**
                        Sabores a Bacalhau 3
❶   Tartaruga   2
❷
                        BARS & CLUBS
                        Azul Profundo   5
Feira   Havana   1
Internacional   República da Cerveja 4
de Lisboa ❸
                        SHOPS
                        Centro Vasco da Gama a

AVENIDA DOM JOÃO II
CAMINHO DA ÁGUA
Garcia de Orta Gardens

0   1 km

Bowling

❹

RUA RECÍPROCA   Pavilhão   Rio Tejo
AV. DO ÍNDICO   Atlântico
Estação
do Oriente
Ⓜ   Centro
Oriente   Vasco   ⓘ Bike
            da Gama   Hire
                       Nautical Centro
AV. DE BERLIM AV. DO PACÍFICO   River Gate
            ⓐ
                       Council of ❺
                       Ministers
            CAMINHO DA ASA
                       Pavilhão
                       de Portugal   Teleférico
                       Olivais
                       Nook   N
Casino   △ Cacilhas
AV. DE ULYSSES   Oceanário   PASSEIO DAS TÁGIDES
AVENIDA DCM JOÃO II

                       Pavilhão do
                       Conhecimento
                       (Ciência Viva)
AV. DE MEDITERRÂNEO   Jardins da Água
                       Teatro   **PARQUE**
                       Camões   **DAS NAÇÕES**

▽ Lisbon

district, featuring an enormous, sagging concrete canopy on its south side. Opposite here is the spaceship-like Pavilhão Atlântico (Atlantic Pavilion; ☎218 918 440, ⓦwww .pavilhaoatlantico.pt), Portugal's largest indoor arena and the venue for major visiting bands and sporting events. The MTV music awards were held here in 2005.

Pavilhão do Conhecimento (Ciência Viva)

☎218 917 100. Tues–Fri 10am–6pm, Sat & Sun 11am–7pm. €6, children under 12 €3. Run by Portugal's Ministry of Science and Technology (which shares the premises), the Knowledge Pavilion, (Live Science), hosts changing exhibitions on subjects like 3D animation and the latest computer technology. The

138

permanent exhibits aimed at children – from flight simulators to holograms – are particularly good and there's also a cybercafé offering free Internet access.

Jardins da Água

The Jardins da Água (Water Gardens), crisscrossed by waterways and ponds, are based on the stages of a river's drainage pattern, from stream to estuary. It is not huge, but linked by stepping stones, and there are enough gushing fountains, water gadgets and pumps to keep children occupied for hours.

Oceanário

☎218 917 002, 🌐www.oceanario.pt. Daily 10am–7pm. €10.50, children under 12 €5.25. Designed by Peter Chermaeff and looking like something off the set of a James Bond film, the Oceanário de Lisboa (Lisbon Oceanarium), Europe's second largest, contains some 8,000 fish and marine animals representing 450 species. Its main feature is the enormous central tank, the size of four Olympic-sized swimming pools, which you can look into from different levels for close-up, top-to-bottom views of the sharks, which circle the main body of the water, down to the rays burying themselves into the sand. Almost more impressive, though, are the recreations of various ocean ecosystems, such as the Antarctic tank, containing frolicking penguins, and the Pacific tank, where otters bob about in the rock pools. On a darkened lower level, smaller tanks contain shoals of brightly coloured tropical fish and other warm-water creatures. Find a window free of school parties and the whole experience becomes the closest you'll get to deep-sea diving without getting wet.

The teleférico and the Jardins da Orta

Mon–Fri 11am–7pm, Sat & Sun 10am–8pm. €3.50 one-way, €5.50 return. Children under 12 €1.80 single, €3.50 return. The ski-lift-style *teleférico* (cable car) rises up to 20m as it shuttles you over Olivais Docks to the northern side of the Parque, giving commanding views over the site on the way. It drops down to the Garcia da Orta gardens, containing exotic trees from Portugal's former colonies. Behind the gardens, Rua

Parque das Nações PLACES

▲ OCEANÁRIO

Pimenta is lined with a motley collection of international restaurants, from Irish to Israeli.

Torre Vasco da Gama

Once an integral part of an oil refinery, the Torre Vasco da Gama (Vasco da Gama Tower) is, at 145m high, Lisbon's tallest structure. The tower is currently being converted into a five-star hotel.

Parque do Tejo

Spreading along the waterfront for two kilometers right up to the Vasco da Gama bridge, Parque do Tejo is Lisbon's newest park, with bike trails and riverside walks. It's a great spot for a picnic – picnic supplies are available from the supermarkets in the Vasco da Gama shopping centre and bike hire from the Sony Plaza.

Feira Internacional de Lisboa

☏ 218 921 500, ⓦ www.fil.pt. Opposite Sony Plaza, Lisbon's trade fair hall, the Feira Internacional de Lisboa (FIL), hosts various events, including a handicrafts fair displaying ceramics and crafts from around the country (usually in July).

Casino

☏ 218 929 000. The brand-new state-of-the-art casino opened in 2006. Along with the usual casino attractions, the stunning space – with its glass cylinder entrance hall – also hosts top shows from Broadway and London as well as major concerts in the performance hall, which has a retractable roof.

Shops

Centro Vasco da Gama

Avda D. João II ☏ 218 930 601,

▲ VASCO DA GAMA SHOPPING COMPLEX

ⓦ www.centrovascodagama.pt. Daily 10am–midnight. Three floors of local and international stores are housed under a glass roof, washed by permanently running water; international branches include Zara, Pierre Cardin, Massimo Dutti and C&A and local sports and book shops also feature. There are also various fast-food outlets, ten cinema screens, children's areas and a huge Continente supermarket on the lower floor.

Freeport

Over the river in Alcochete; reached by bus #431 or 432 from Oriente station. Daily 10am–midnight. Giant designer-discount complex a twenty-minute bus ride from the park, boasting over two hundred shops. International names include Hugo Boss, Zara, Versace, Burberry, Gucci and Pierre Cardin, supported by some 40 restaurants, bars and cafés. The complex has also become a venue for touring bands – Ronan Keating, Sugababes, Jamie Callum and Craig David have all appeared here.

Restaurants

Sabores a Bacalhau
Rua da Pimenta 47 ☎218 957 290. Mon & Wed–Sun noon–11pm. This is an unassuming place with outdoor tables, whose name translates as "tastes of dried cod". It offers around 14 of the alleged 365 *bacalhau* dishes that you can sample, at good value prices.

Tartaruga
Rua da Pimenta 95 ☎218 957 499. Tues–Sun noon–5am. Standard Portuguese fare with a few tasty pasta dishes too, and outdoor seats facing the gardens. On Fridays and Saturdays the inside switches to a dance bar after midnight, when the decor appears increasingly lurid.

Bars and clubs

Azul Profundo
Doca da Olivais. Daily 10am–1am, closes 7pm from Oct–April. Sunny esplanade bar overlooking the glittering docks. Offers a good range of snacks, fruit juices and fantastic *caipirinha* cocktails.

Havana
Rua da Pimenta 115–117. Daily noon–4am, closed Tues Oct–April. Lively

▲ VIEW OVER OLIVAIS DOCK

Cuban bar with an airy interior and outdoor seating. The pulsating Latin sounds get progressively louder after 11pm, when it turns into more of a club until 4am.

República da Cerveja
Passeio das Tágides 2–26 ☎218 922 590. Daily 12.30pm–1am. In a great position close to the water's edge and facing the Vasco da Gama bridge, this modern bar-restaurant specializes in some fine international beers, though sticking to the local Superbock will save a few euros. Steaks and German cuisine are also on offer, and there's live music Thursday to Saturday.

Sintra

If you make just one day-trip during your stay in Lisbon, choose the ride out to the beautiful hilltop town of Sintra, the former summer residence of Portuguese royalty and a UNESCO World Heritage Site since 1995. Not only does the town boast two of Portugal's most extraordinary palaces, it also contains a semi-tropical garden, a Moorish castle with breathtaking views over Lisbon, and one of the best modern-art museums in the Iberian peninsula. Looping around a series of green, wooded ravines and with a climate that encourages moss and ferns to grow from every nook and cranny, Sintra consists of three separate districts. Sintra-Vila is the oldest part, with many of the town's attractions close to its central square, the Praça da República; Estefânia, a ten-minute walk to the east, is where trains from Lisbon pull in; while São Pedro – best visited on the eve of São Pedro, the main saint's day (June 28), and for its market on the second and fourth Sunday of the month – lies to the south, and is well known for its antique shops.

Palácio Nacional

Largo da Rainha Dona Amélia ☏219 106 840. Mon, Tues & Thurs–Sun 10am–5.30pm. €4, free Sun 10am–2pm. Best seen early or late in the day to avoid the crowds, the extraordinary Palácio Nacional was probably already in existence at the time of the Moors. It takes its present form from the rebuilding of Dom João I (1385–1433) and his successor, Dom Manuel I, the chief royal beneficiary of Vasco da Gama's explorations. Its exterior style is an amalgam of Gothic – featuring impressive battlements – and Manueline,

Visiting Sintra

Sintra is served by regular trains from Lisbon's **Rossio, Entre Campos** and **Sete Rios** station (every 15–20min; 45min; €1.50 single). To see the area around Sintra, including the coast, consider a **Day-rover (Turístico Diário) ticket** on the local Scotturb buses (Ⓦwww.scotturb.com; €8.50, or €12 to include trains to and from Lisbon). Alternatively, **bus #434** takes a circular route from Sintra station or Sintra-Vila to most of the sites mentioned in this chapter (every 40min; €3.85) and allows you to get on and off whenever you like on the circuit. Another option is the toy train (departures roughly hourly from 10am–5pm, day ticket €5), which shuttles from the Palácio Nacional to Monserrate via Quinta da Regaleira. Finally, quaint old trams shuttle from outside the Museu de Arte Moderna to the coastal resort of Praia das Maçãs via Colares (Fri–Sun at 10am, noon, 2pm & 3.30pm; return at 11am, 1pm, 2.55pm & 4.45pm, 45 mins. €2 single. Also Tues–Thurs for group bookings, ☏219 233 919.

Strange happenings in Sintra

Sintra was a centre for cult worship for centuries: the early Celts named it Mountain of the Moon after their Moon god, and the hills are scattered with alleged ley lines and mysterious tombs. Locals say batteries drain in the area noticeably faster than anywhere else and light bulbs seem to pop with monotonous regularity. Some claim this is because of the angle of iron in the rocks, others that it is all part of the mystical powers that lurk in Sintra's hills and valleys. There are certainly plenty of geographical and meteorological quirks. In the woods around Capuchos (see p.150) house-sized boulders litter the landscape as if thrown by giants, while a white cloud – affectionately known as the queen's fart – regularly hovers over Sintra's palaces even on the clearest summer day. Exterior walls seem to merge with the landscape as they are quickly smothered in a thick layer of ferns, lichens and moss. Its castles, palaces, mansions and follies shelter tales of Masonic rites, insanity and eccentricity that are as fantastical as the buildings themselves.

tempered inside by a good deal of Moorish influence, adapted over the centuries by a succession of royal occupants. Sadly, after the fall of the monarchy in 1910, most of the surrounding walls and medieval houses were destroyed. Highlights on the lower floor include the Manueline Sala dos Cisnes, so-called for the swans (*cisnes*) on its ceiling, and the Sala das Pegas, which takes its

▼ CASTELO DOS MOUROS WALLS

name from the flock of magpies (*pegas*) painted on the frieze and ceiling – João I, caught in the act of kissing a lady-in-waiting by his queen, reputedly had the room decorated with as many magpies as there were women at court, to imply they were all magpie-like gossips.

Best of the upper floor is the gallery above the palace chapel. Beyond, a succession of state rooms finishes with the Sala das Brasões, its domed and coffered ceiling emblazoned with the arms of 72 noble families. Finally, don't miss the kitchens, whose roofs taper into the giant chimneys that are the palace's distinguishing features. The Palace also hosts events for the Sintra Music Festival (see p186).

Museu do Brinquedo

Rua Visconde de Monserrate 29
☏ 219 242 171, ⊛ www.museu-do-brinquedo.pt. Tues–Sun 10am–6pm. €3, children under 12 €1.50.
Housed in a former fire station, the Museu do Brinquedo – a fascinating private toy collection – is a great place for children. The huge array of toys exhibited over three floors is somewhat confusingly labelled, but look out for the

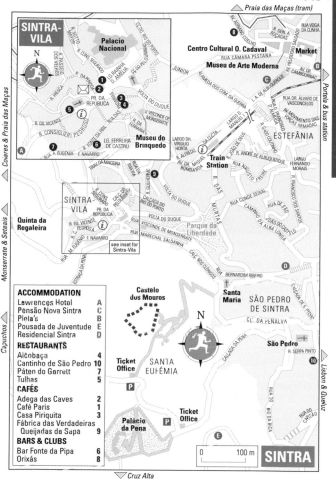

Praia das Maças (tram)

SINTRA-VILA

Palacio Nacional

Centro Cultural O. Cadaval

Market

Museu de Arte Moderna

Coxres & Praia das Maças

Monserrate & Setais

Cajuchos

Portela & bus station

Museu do Brinquedo

Train Station

ESTEFÂNIA

SINTRA-VILA

Quinta da Regaleira

Parque da Liberdade

see inset for Sintra-Vila

Santa Maria

SÃO PEDRO DE SINTRA

São Pedro

ACCOMMODATION
Lawrences Hotel — A
Pensão Nova Sintra — C
Piela's — B
Pousada de Juventude — E
Residencial Sintra — D

RESTAURANTS
Alcobaça — 4
Cantinho de São Pedro — 10
Páten do Garrett — 7
Tulhas — 5

CAFÉS
Adega das Caves — 2
Café Paris — 1
Casa Piriquita — 3
Fábrica das Verdadeiras Queijadas da Sapa — 9

BARS & CLUBS
Bar Fonte da Pipa — 6
Orixás — 8

Castelo dos Mouros

SANTA EUFÉMIA

Ticket Office

Ticket Office

Palácio da Pena

Lisbon & Queluz

0   100 m

SINTRA

Cruz Alta

3000-year-old stone Egyptian toys on the first floor, the 1930s Hornby trains and some of the first-ever toy cars, produced in Germany in the early 1900s'. There are cases of soldiers numerous enough to scare a real army, early Portuguese toys including a selection of 1930s' beach toys, wooden toys from Senegal, wire bicycles from Zimbabwe, and a top floor stuffed with dolls and doll's house furniture. There's also a café and a small play area for young children.

Castelo dos Mouros

☎ 219 237 300. Daily: May–Oct 9am–7pm; Nov–April 9.30am–6pm; last entry 1hr before closing. €3.50.
Reached on bus #434, or a steep drive up on the road to Palácio da Pena, the ruined ramparts of the Castelo dos Mouros are truly spectacular.

▲ ONE OF SINTRA'S NATURAL FOUNTAINS

Built in the ninth century, the castle was taken in 1147 by Afonso Henriques, with the aid of Scandinavian Crusaders. The castle walls were allowed to fall into disrepair over subsequent centuries, though they were restored in the mid-nineteenth century under the orders of Ferdinand II. The Moorish castle spans – and is partly built into – two rocky pinnacles, with the remains of a mosque spread midway between the fortifications, and the views from up here are extraordinary: south beyond Lisbon to the Serra da Arrábida, west to Cabo da Roca and north to the Berlenga islands.

If you want to walk from Sintra, take Calçada dos Clérigos, near the church of Santa Maria. From here, a stone pathway leads all the way up to the lower slopes, where you can see a Moorish grain silo and a ruined twelfth-century church. To enter the castle itself, you'll need to walk further along the path to buy a ticket from the road exit and double back to the castle.

Palácio da Pena

Estrada da Pena ☎ 219 105 340. Tues–Sun: end-June to mid-Sept 10am–7pm; mid-Sept to end-June 10am–5.30pm; last entry 1hr before closing. Palace and gardens €6, gardens only €3.50. Bus #434 stops opposite the lower entrance to Parque da Pena, a stretch of rambling woodland with a scattering of lakes and follies. At the top of the park, about twenty minutes' walk from the entrance or a short ride on a shuttle bus (€1.50 return), looms the fabulous Palácio da Pena, a wild fantasy of domes, towers, ramparts and walkways, approached through mock-Manueline gateways and a drawbridge that does not draw. A compelling riot of kitsch, the palace was built in the 1840s to the specifications of Ferdinand of Saxe-Coburg-Gotha, husband of Queen Maria II, with the help of the German architect, Baron Eschwege. The interior is preserved exactly as it was left by the royal family when it fled Portugal in 1910. The result is fascinating: rooms of stone decorated to look like wood, statues of turbaned Moors nonchalantly holding electric chandeliers – it's all here. Of an original convent, founded in the early sixteenth century to celebrate the first sight of Vasco da Gama's returning fleet, only a beautiful, tiled chapel and serene Manueline cloister have been retained.

Above Pena, a marked footpath climbs in thirty minutes or so to the **Cruz Alta**, the highest point of the Serra de Sintra, at 529m.

Quinta da Regaleira

Daily: Feb–April & Oct 10am–6.30pm; May–Sept 10am–8pm; Nov–Jan

10am–5.30pm. Tours (90min, available in English) every 30min–60min; advance booking essential on ☎219 106 650; €10. Unguided visits €5. The Quinta da Regaleira, a UNESCO World Heritage site, is one of Sintra's most elaborate estates. It was designed at the end of the nineteenth century by Italian architect and theatrical set designer Luigi Manini for wealthy Brazilian merchant António Augusto Carvalho Monteiro. Manini's penchant for the dramatic is obvious: the principal building, the mock-Manueline Palácio dos Milhões, sprouts turrets and towers, though the interior is sparse apart from some elaborate Rococo wooden ceilings and impressive Art Nouveau tiles. It is best to take a tour to get the full flavour of the place, though you are free to look around where you want unguided.

The surrounding gardens shelter fountains, terraces, lakes and grottoes, with the highlight being the Initiation Well, inspired by the initiation practices of the Knights Templar and the Freemasons. Entering via a Harry Potter-style revolving stone door, you walk down a moss-covered spiral staircase to the foot of the well and through a tunnel, which eventually resurfaces at the edge of a lake (though in winter you exit from a shorter tunnel so as not to disturb a colony of hibernating bats). In summer, the gardens host occasional performances of live music, usually classical or jazz.

Sintra Museu de Arte Moderna

Avenida Heliodoro Salgado ☎219 248 170, ⓦ www.berardocollection.com. Tues–Sun 10am–6pm. €3, free Sun 10am 2am. The Museu de Arte Moderna houses one of Iberia's best collections of modern art, amassed by Madeiran tobacco magnate Joe Berardo. Located in Sintra's former casino, the collection spreads over three floors, displaying the main modern movements, including pop art, minimalism, kinetic and conceptual art. The collection is so huge that exhibits change every two months as there is only space to show twenty works at any one time, alongside temporary exhibits. Depending on when you visit, you might see works by Jackson Pollock, David Hockney, Roy Lichtenstein and Andy Warhol, including his wonderful portrait of Judy Garland. Lovers of kitsch will enjoy both Jeff Koons' sculptures of a poodle and Bobtail the sheepdog.

♥ QUINTA DA REGALEIRA

▲ LOCAL *QUEIJADAS* (SWEET CHEESECAKES)

Cafés

Adega das Caves
Rua da Pendoa 2. ☎ 219 239 848.
Daily 9am–2am. Bustling café-
bar in the basement of *Café
Paris*, (see below) attracting a
predominantly local and youthful
clientele; snacks, baguettes and
pizzas for around €6.

Café Paris
Largo Rainha D. Amélia ☎ 219 232
375. Daily 8am–midnight. This
attractive blue-tiled café is the
highest-profile in town, which
means steep prices for not
especially exciting food,
although it is a great place to
sit and nurse a drink in the
sun. If you do want to eat,
reservations are advised in
high season. Tourist menu is
around €25.

Casa Piriquita
Rua das Padarias 1. Mon, Tues &
Thurs–Sun 9am–midnight. Cosy
tea-room and bakery, which
can get busy with locals
queueing to buy *queijadas da
Sintra* (sweet cheesecakes)
and other pastries. Further up

the hill at no. 18 there's
another, more modern branch,
Piriquita Dois (closed Tues),
which boasts a big outdoor
terrace.

Fábrica das Verdadeiras
Queijadas da Sapa
Volta do Duche 12. Tues–Sun 9am–
7pm. This old-fashioned café is
famed for its traditional
queijadas, which have been made
on the premises for over a
century. It's a bit dingy inside, so
it's best to buy takeaways to
sustain you on your walk to the
centre.

▼ LAWRENCE'S HOTEL (SEE P.174)

Restaurants

Alcobaça

Rua das Padarias 7–11 ☎219 231 651. Daily noon–4.30pm & 7pm–midnight. There's friendly service in the plain tiled dining room, and large servings of grilled chicken, sardine *cataplana* and pasta dishes for €15–20 a head. Also does a fine sangria.

Cantinho de São Pedro

Praça D. Fernando II 18, São Pedro de Sintra ☎219 230 267. Daily 12.30–3pm & 7.30–11pm. Large restaurant with bare stone walls overlooking an attractive courtyard just off São Pedro's main square. Slightly formal service but excellent food at reasonable prices. Try the daily specials which are usually good value. On cool evenings a log fire keeps things cosy.

Páteo do Garrett

Rua Maria Eugénia Reis F. Navarro 7 ☎219 243 380. Mon, Tues & Thurs–Sun 11am–11pm; Jan–April 11am–2pm. Although this café-restaurant has a dark, dim interior, it's also got a lovely sunny patio offering fine views over the village. Serves standard Portuguese fare from around €12, or just pop in for a drink.

Tulhas

Rua Gil Vicente 4 ☎219 232 378. Mon, Tues & Thurs–Sun noon–3.30pm & 7–10pm. Imaginative cooking in a fine building converted from old grain silos. The giant mixed grills at €22 for two people will keep carnivores more than happy, while the weekend specials are usually excellent. Reservations are advised.

Bars and clubs

Bar Fonte da Pipa

Rua Fonte da Pipa 11–13 ☎219 234 437. Daily 9pm–2am. Laid-back bar attracting a sophisticated clientele, with low lighting and comfy chairs. It's up the hill from *Casa da Piriquita*, next to the lovely ornate fountain (*fonte*) that the street is named after.

Orixás

Avda Adriano Coelho 7 ☎219 241 672. Tues–Fri 4pm–midnight, Sat & Sun noon–4pm & 8pm–midnight. Brazilian bar, restaurant, music venue and art gallery housed in a lovely building complete with waterfalls and outdoor terrace, on the road behind the Museu de Arte Moderna. Go for the buffet to sample its range of Brazilian specialities; it costs around €30, but with live Brazilian music thrown in, that's not bad value.

▲ BAR FONTE DA PIPA

PLACES Sintra

The Sintra coast, Queluz and around

The beautiful hills, woodlands and craggy coastline around Sintra make up the Parque Natural Sintra-Cascais, within which development is restricted. West of Sintra, beyond the fantastic gardens of Monserrate, the wine-producing village of Colares and the extraordinary Convento dos Capuchos, a series of small-scale coastal resorts stretches north of Cabo da Roca (Cape of Rock), mainland Europe's most westerly point. The sands make an attractive destination for an afternoon out (or even an overnight stop), but note that all the beaches have dangerous currents. Exactly halfway between Lisbon and Sintra, the eighteenth-century Rococo Palácio de Queluz provides a rewarding break in your journey.

Monserrate

Estrada da Monserrate ☎ 219 237 300. Daily: May–Sept 9am–7pm; Oct–April 9.30am–6pm. €3.50. Guided tours to palace daily at 10am & 3pm, €7. Toy train from Sintra (see p142) €5, or return taxi from Sintra with 1hr stopover costs around €25. The charm of Monserrate, a Victorian folly-like mansion set in a vast botanical park of exotic trees and subtropical shrubs and plants, is immeasurably enhanced by the fact that it's only partially maintained. The name most associated with Monserrate is that of William Beckford, the wealthiest untitled Englishman of his age, who rented Monserrate from 1793 to 1799, having been forced to flee Britain after he was caught in a compromising position with a sixteen-year-old boy. Setting about improving the place, he landscaped a waterfall and even imported a flock of sheep from his estate at Fonthill, Wiltshire.

Half a century later, a second immensely rich Englishman, Sir Francis Cook, bought the estate. His fantasies were scarcely less ambitious. Cook imported the head gardener from Kew to lay out succulents and water plants, tropical ferns and palms, and just

▼ MONSERRATE GARDENS

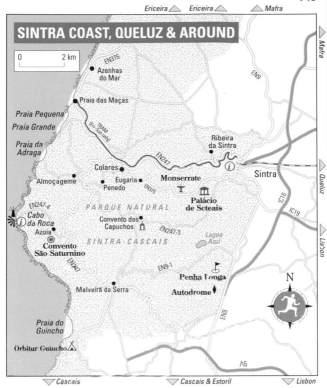

SINTRA COAST, QUELUZ & AROUND

about every known conifer. For a time Monserrate boasted the only lawn in Iberia and it remains one of Europe's most richly stocked gardens, with over a thousand different species of subtropical trees and plants.

Cook's main legacy was the construction of a great Victorian palace inspired by Brighton Pavilion. You can visit sections of the partly restored palace on daily tours (pre-booking essential on ☎219 237 300), though until renovation is completed, the most impressive part remains the exterior, with its mix of Moorish and Italian decoration – the dome is modelled on the Duomo in Florence.

Colares

Bus #403 from Sintra or Cascais train stations (every 90min) or #441 from Sintra; or Praia das Maças tram from Sintra Estefânia (see p142). Twenty minutes northwest of Sintra, this wealthy village is famed for its rich red wine made from grapes harvested from the ancient vines grown in the local sandy soil. The producer Adega Regional de Colares (☎219 288 082) hosts occasional tastings, concerts and exhibitions. For superb views back towards Sintra, head uphill following the sign "Penedo".

Azenhas do Mar

Bus #441 from Sintra (every 1–2hr; 40min). Whitewashed cottages tumble down the steep cliff face

▲ AZENHAS DO MAR

at the pretty village of Azenhas do Mar. The beach is small, but there are artificial seawater pools for swimming in when the sea is too rough.

Praia das Maçãs

Bus #441 from Sintra (every 1–2hr; 30min); or Praia das Maças tram from Sintra (see p142). The largest and liveliest resort on this stretch, Praia das Maçãs is also the easiest to reach from Sintra – take the tram for the most enjoyable journey. Along with a big swath of sand, Praia das Maçãs has an array of bars and restaurants to suit all budgets.

Praia Grande

Bus #441 from Sintra (every 1–2hr; 25min). Set in a wide, sandy cliff-backed bay, this is one of the best and safest beaches on the Sintra coast, though its breakers attract surfers aplenty. In August the World Bodyboarding Championships are held here, along with games such as volleyball and beach rugby. Plenty of inexpensive cafés and restaurants are spread out along the beachside road.

Praia da Adraga

No public transport; by car, follow the signs from the village of Almoçageme. Praia da Adraga was flatteringly voted one of Europe's best beaches by a British newspaper; the unspoilt, cliff-backed, sandy bay with just one beach restaurant is certainly far quieter than the other resorts, but it takes the full brunt of the Atlantic, so you'll need to take great care when swimming.

Cabo da Roca

Bus #403 from Sintra or Cascais train stations (every 90min; 45min). Little more than a windswept rocky cape with a lighthouse, this is the most westerly point in mainland Europe, which guarantees a steady stream of visitors – get there early to avoid the coach parties. You can soak up the views from the café-restaurant and handicraft shop (daily 9.30am–7.30pm) and buy a certificate to prove you've been here at the little tourist office (daily 9am–6.30pm, ☎219 280 081).

Convento dos Capuchos

45min guided tours only (available in English); ☎219 237 300; daily: May–Oct 9am–7pm every 30min; Nov–Feb 10am–4.30pm 6 tours daily; March–April 9.30am–6pm roughly hourly. €3.50. Advance booking essential. No public transport. A return taxi from Sintra with a 1hr stopover costs around €30. If you have your own transport, don't miss a trip to the Convento dos Capuchos, an extraordinary hermitage with tiny, dwarf-like cells cut from the rock and lined with cork – hence its popular name of the Cork Convent. It was occupied for three hundred years until being finally abandoned in 1834 by its seven remaining monks, who must have found the gloomy warren of rooms and corridors too much to maintain. Some rooms – the penitents' cells – can only be entered by crawling through 70cm-high doors; here, and on every other ceiling, doorframe and lintel, are attached panels of cork, taken from the surrounding woods. Elsewhere, you'll come across a washroom, kitchen, refectory, tiny chapels, and even a bread oven set apart from the main complex.

Penha Longa Golf Club

Estrada da Lagoa Azul-Linhó ☎219 249 031, ⓦwww.penhalonga.com. Mon–Fri €90 per round, Sat & Sun €105. Golf club hire from €45. One of Portugal's most famous golf courses, the upmarket Penha Longa Golf Club is set in a former fourteenth-century monastic estate, later used as a royal palace. Designed by famous English-born golf architect Robert Trent Jones, the course has superb views towards the sea and has hosted the Portuguese Open. Not surprisingly, it's best to book in advance to be sure of a game; note that a handicap of 28 is required. For details of the area's other courses, see ⓦwww .estorilsintragolf.com.pt.

Palácio de Queluz

☎214 343 860. Mon & Wed–Sun 9.30am–5pm. €4, free Sun 10am–2pm. Train from Sintra or Lisbon's Rossio, Entre Campos or Sete Rios stations to Queluz-Belas (every 15–20min; 20min; €1 single). Commissioned in 1747 and long-used as the summer residence for royals, the Palácio de Queluz is the country's finest example of Rococo architecture. Although its low, pink-washed wings and extensive eighteenth-century formal gardens are preserved as a museum, the palace is still pressed into service to accommodate state guests and dignitaries. It was built by Dom Pedro III, husband and

PLACES The Sintra coast, Queluz and around

▼ PRAIA GRANDE

regent to his niece, Queen Maria I. Maria lived here throughout her 39-year reign (1777–1816), for the last 27 years of which she was quite mad, following the death of her eldest son, José.

Visitors first enter the Throne Room, which is lined with mirrors surmounted by paintings and golden flourishes. Beyond is the more conservative Music Chamber with its portrait of Queen Maria above a French grand piano. Another wing comprises an elegant suite of smoking, coffee and dining rooms, as well as the Ambassador's Chamber, where diplomats and foreign ministers were received during the nineteenth century. One of the most pleasing rooms is the simple Dressing Room, with its geometric inlaid wooden floor and intricate ceiling.

Entry to the formal gardens is included in the ticket price. From May to October (except Aug) there's a display of Portuguese horsemanship here every Wednesday at 11am, and the palace also hosts events for the Sintra music festival (see p.186).

Restaurants

Colares Velho
Largo Dr Carlos de Franca 1–4, Colares ☎219 292 406. Wed–Sat 11am–11pm, Sun 11am–3pm. Delightful upmarket restaurant and teahouse on Colares' tiny main square. The traditional Portuguese cuisine, such as *bacalhau*, starts at around €15, but it's worth the price (in autumn, game is a speciality); alternatively, just pop in for tea and cakes.

▲ COLARES VELHO RESTAURANT

Cozinha Velha
Palácio de Queluz ☎214 350 232. Daily 12.30–3pm & 7.30–10pm. You can still eat in the original kitchen of the Queluz palace, although the food doesn't always live up to its setting and you're looking at around €30 a head for a full meal.

O Loureiro
Esplanada Vasco da Gama, Praia das Maçãs ☎219 292 442. Mon–Wed & Fri–Sun 11am–3pm & 7–11pm. In a prime location overlooking the beach, this is the best place to try the local fresh fish and seafood; the grilled squid is always a good and inexpensive choice.

Bars

Maças Club
Rua Pedro Álvaro Cabral 2–12, Praia das Maçãs ☎219 292 024. Daily 10am–6am. With an outdoor terrace facing the sands, this is the ideal spot for a cool drink, sandwich or ice cream. The action moves upstairs as the evening progresses, with dance music until the small hours.

The Cascais coast

Lisbon's most accessible coastline lies just beyond the point where the Tejo flows into the Atlantic at the popular resorts along the Cascais coast. With its grandiose villas, luxury hotels and top-rated golf courses, Estoril (pronounced é-stril) has pretensions towards being a Portuguese Riviera, but it lacks the character and buzz of neighbouring Cascais (pronounced cash-kaysh), which has a much younger and less exclusive feel and makes the better day-trip of the two. Getting to the resorts is half the fun – from the city centre, trains from Cais do Sodré (every 20min; 35min to Estoril, 40min to Cascais; €1.50 single) wend along the shore – at times so close to the water that waves almost break over the tracks. There are also regular buses to and from Sintra and Lisbon airport. Sadly, the water along this stretch is not particularly clean until you get beyond Cascais to the impressive beach of Guincho.

Estoril

Estoril's town centre is focused on the leafy **Parque do Estoril**, surrounded by bars and restaurants. At the top end of the park is Europe's biggest **casino** (Tues–Sat 3pm–3am; free; semi-formal attire required; ☎214 667 700, ⓦwww.casino-estoril.pt), where James Bond author Ian Fleming gained much of his inspiration for his agents' exploits. The **Feira Internacional Artesanato** – handicrafts and folk music festival – is held nearby in July.

The resort's fine sandy beach, **Praia de Tamariz**, is backed by a **seafront promenade** that stretches all the way northwest to Cascais. A stroll between the two towns is recommended, drifting from beach to bar; the

ORIL

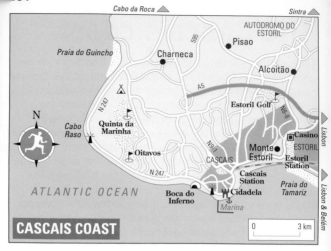

walk takes around twenty minutes. From July to mid-September, a free firework display takes place above the beach every Saturday night at midnight.

Cascais

Many of Cascais' most popular bars and restaurants cluster round the attractive palmtree-lined Largo Luis de Camões, set at one end of Rua Frederico Arouca. Nearby is the lively **fish market** (Mon–Fri), best in the afternoon after the catch comes in.

The old and pretty west side of Cascais town is at its most charming in the streets west of the graceful **Igreja da Assunção** – worth a look inside for its azulejos, which predate the earthquake of 1755. The modern **Museu do Mar** (Tues–Sun 10am–5pm; €1.65; ☎214 825 400) is an engaging little collection of items showing the town's relationship with the sea, with model boats, naval costumes and evocative photos of old Cascais.

The delightful **Parque Municipal da Gandarinha**, filled with exotic trees, picnic tables and a small lake, as well as a mini zoo and playground, makes a welcome escape from the beach crowds. In one corner of the park stands the beautiful mansion of the nineteenth-century Count of Guimarães, preserved complete with its fittings as the **Museu Biblioteca Conde Castro Guimarães** (Tues–Sun 10am–5pm; tours €1.65; ☎214 825 407).

To the east, the walls of Cascais' largely seventeenth-century fortress (closed to the public) now guard the entrance to the **Marina de Cascais**, an enclave of expensive yachts serviced by restaurants, bars and boutiques.

Cascais beaches

Cascais's largest beach, **Praia da Conceição**, lies east of Rua Frederico Arouca – Cascais' main mosaic-paved pedestrian thoroughfare – and is the best place to lounge on the sands

You can also hire pedaloes or go windsurfing or waterskiing from here. The smaller beaches of **Praia da Rainha** and **Praia da Ribeira** are off the central stretch of town surrounded by rock formations which are great for clambering over and using as diving platforms. To the south of town, overlooked by a lighthouse and below a low cliff, is the little beach of **Praia de Santa Marta**, with a pleasant café on a terrace above the sands; it's a tranquil spot, though signs advise against swimming here.

Boca do Inferno

It's about twenty minutes' walk west from Cascais along the coastal road to the Boca do Inferno – the "Mouth of Hell" – where waves crash against caves in the cliff face. The viewpoints above are always packed with tourists, but the whole affair is rather unimpressive, except in stormy weather.

Praia do Guincho

There are buses every one or two hours from Cascais bus station to Praia do Guincho, 6km west, a great sweeping beach with body-crushing Atlantic rollers. The water is clean and it's a superb place to surf or windsurf – windsurfing championships are usually held here in August – but the undertow is notoriously strong and people are drowned almost every year. The beach and the coastal approach road is flanked by half a dozen large terrace-restaurants, all with fish-dominated menus.

Cafés

Esplanada Santa Marta

Praia de Santa Marta, Cascais. Tues–Sat 10am–10pm. One of the best places to enjoy charcoal-grilled fish, which is served on a tiny terrace overlooking the sea and the little beach.

Music Bar

Largo da Praia da Rainha 121, Cascais. May–Sept daily 10am–10pm; Oct–April closed Mon. One of the few café-bars in Cascais with fine sea views. It's a fine spot to have a sunset beer, and the outside tables on the patio above the beach are packed

A DA CONCEIÇÃO, CASCAIS

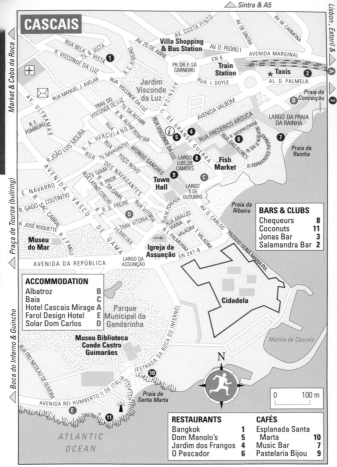

Left margin references:
Market & Cabo da Roca ◁
Praça de Touros (bullring) ◁
Boca do Inferno & Guincho ◁

Right margin:
Lisbon, Estoril & ▷

CASCAIS

Map labels:
Sintra & A5
AV. COSTA PINTO
AV. M CARRAINA
AV. DE SINTRA
RUA BELA V. VISTA
R. V. S VISTA
R. VISCONDE DA LUZ
AV. 25 DE ABRIL
Villa Shopping & Bus Station
AV. D. PEDRO I
EN 6
PR. DR. F. SÁ CARNEIRO
AVENIDA MARGINAL
Train Station
RUA I. DOYLE
★ Taxis
AL. D. PALMELA
Praia da Conceição
RUA MANUEL J. AVELAR
Jardim Visconde da Luz
AV. ULTRAMAR
R.F. POMBEIRO
TRAV. DO VISCONDE DE LUZ
R. N. ALFARROBEIRA
AVENIDA VALBOM
LARGO DA PRAIA DA RAINHA
R. TV DA ALFARR
RUA VISCONDE DA LUZ
AVENIDA C. DE GRANDE GUERRA
RUA FREDERICO AROUCA
R. DA MISERICÓRDIA
RUA DAS FLORES
R. JOÃO LUIS MOURA
R. A. HERCULANO
RUA NAVAGANTES
RUA AFONSO SANCHES
LARGO DE LUIS DE CAMÕES
Fish Market
R. FERNANDES
Praia da Rainha
AVENIDA VASCO
E. NAVARRO
R. GAGO COUTINHO
SAC. CABRAL
RUA TV GAMA-P
R. PRIOR
POÇO NOVO
RUA DOS NAVAGANTES
RUA LATINO CORHO
R. DA GAMA
RUA VITORIA
Town Hall
LARGO 5 DE OUTUBRO
Praia da Ribeira
R. JOSÉ ROQUETTE
R.J.P. NELO
D. FERREIRA
TRAV. VITORIA
RUA ARAUJO VIANA
RUA ROSADA
R. T VALADIM
R. L PALMEIRA
T. VALADIM
AV. D. CARLOS
PASSEIO DONA MARIA PIA
Museu do Mar
AVENIDA DA REPÚBLICA
LARGO DA ASSUNÇÃO
Igreja da Assunção
EN 247-8

BARS & CLUBS
Chequeurs	8
Coconuts	11
Jonas Bar	3
Salamandra Bar	2

Cidadela
Marina de Cascais

ACCOMMODATION
Albatroz	B
Baia	C
Hotel Cascais Mirage	A
Farol Design Hotel	E
Solar Dom Carlos	D

Parque Municipal da Gandarinha

Museu Biblioteca Conde Castro Guimarães

ESTRADA DA BOCA DO INFERNO
RUA FREDERICO DE OLIVEIRA
AVENIDA REI HUMBERTO II DE ITÁLIA
Praia de Santa Marta

N

0   100 m

ATLANTIC OCEAN

RESTAURANTS		**CAFÉS**	
Bangkok	1	Esplanada Santa Marta	10
Dom Manolo's	5	Music Bar	7
Jardim dos Frangos	4	Pastelaria Bijou	9
O Pescador	6		

throughout the day. It also does decent, moderately priced fish and grilled meats from around €10.

Pastelaria Bijou

Rua Rigimento XIX 55, off Largo Luís de Camões, Cascais. Daily 9am–9pm. Simple café in a pretty tiled building with outside seats on the square. One of the cheapest places round here for lunches, snacks, pastries or drinks.

Restaurants

Bangkok

Rua Bela Vista 6, Cascais ☎214 847 600. Daily 12.30–3pm & 7.30–11pm. Sublime Thai cooking in a traditional Cascais town house, beautifully decorated with inlaid wood and Oriental furnishings. This place is popular, attracting media stars and politicians, so it's best to reserve in advance. Highlights include lobster in curry past and the assorted Thai snacks; expect to pay upwards of €30 a head if you choose seafood mains, though you can eat for less much if you choose carefully.

Dom Manolo's

Avda Com. Grande Guerra 11, Cascais ☎ 214 831 126. Daily 10am–midnight. Busy grill-house where superb chicken and chips, salad, local wine and home-made dessert will come to around €15.

English Bar/Cimas

Avda Sabóia 9, Monte Estoril (signed just northwest of the train station, around 10min from the centre of Estoril) ☎ 214 680 413. Mon–Sat 12.30–4pm & 7.30–11pm. Despite the name, this is actually one of the region's best restaurants. Named after the Englishman who built the mansion in the 1940s, it has been run by the same Hispano-Portuguese family since 1952. The sumptuous wood-panelled decor, sea views and top-quality fish, meat and game have attracted leading politicians, journalists and even Spanish royalty; not surprisingly, bills are usually over €30 a head.

Jardim dos Frangos

Avda Com. Grande Guerra 66, Cascais. Daily 10am–midnight. Permanently buzzing with people and sizzling with the speciality, bargain grilled chicken, which is devoured by the plateful at indoor and outdoor tables.

Muchaxo

Praia do Guincho ☎ 214 870 221. Daily noon–3.30pm & 7.30–10.30pm. This restaurant, overlooking the crashing waves of Guincho, is ⸺ated one of the best in the ⸺sbon area. A meal will set you

back around €25 a head, but that's not bad value for the delicious Portuguese fish and meat delicacies. Tables at lunch are usually easy to come by, though you might want to book for dinner.

O Pescador

Rua das Flores 10, Cascais ☎ 214 832 054. Mon–Sat 12.30–3pm & 7.30–11pm. One of several restaurants close to the fish market. Small and intimate, this place offers superior fish meals. Good food, smart decor and efficient service; reservations are advised for dinner.

Praia do Tamariz

Praia do Tamariz, Estoril ☎ 214 681 010. Daily 9am–10pm. High-profile restaurant right on the seafront promenade – which makes the fish, meat and pasta dishes pretty good value (mains cost from €15). Also a great spot for a sangria or *caipirinha*.

▼ FISHING AT BOCA DO INFERNO

Bars and clubs

Chequeurs

Largo Luís de Camões 7, Cascais
℗214 830 926. Daily 10am–2am. An
English-style pub that fills up
early with a good-time crowd; it
serves so-so meals, too, and
shows live soccer on TV, though
most people come for drinks at
tables outside in the attractive
square

Coconuts

Avda Rei Humberto II de Itália 7,
Cascais ℗214 844 109, ⓦwww.nuts-
club.com. Wed–Sat 11pm–4am.
Perennially popular club
attracting trendy locals and
raving tourists. Sea-facing
terrace, karaoke bar and theme
nights (from foam parties to
"ladies" night). Guest DJs appear
on Thursdays.

Jonas Bar

Paredão do Estoril, Monte Estoril. Daily
10am–1am. Right on the seafront
between Cascais and Estoril, this
is a laid-back spot day or night,
selling cocktails, juices and
snacks until the small hours.

Salamandra Bar

Praia da Duquesa, Cascais. ℗214
820 287. Daily 7pm–2am. Next to
the station with a great view of
the seafront, this buzzing bar
has something for everyone,
from bar games to live TV
sports and frequent live music
(jazz and rock). Also serves
snacks.

South of the Tejo

The River Tejo – spanned by the huge Ponte 25 de Abril suspension bridge – separates Lisbon from a string of largely industrial suburbs, but several enjoyable day-trip destinations provide respite from the high-rises. With your own transport, you could take in several of these on a day's circuit from Lisbon. Easiest to reach on a fun ferry ride is Cacilhas, which boasts excellent seafood restaurants and fine views back over the estuary. To the west, Caparica is a high-rise resort on a superb stretch of wave-pounded beach. Further south, your choices are more restricted if you're relying on public transport. Here, there are more fine beaches – like those at Lagoa de Albufeira and Aldeia do Meco – stretching to the southernmost point, at the wild headland of Cabo Espichel. East of here you'll find calmer waters around Sesimbra and the Parque Natural da Arrábida, a craggy mountain range fronted by some superb beaches.

Cacilhas and Almada

Ferries from Cais do Sodré (every 10min, 5.35am–2.30am; €0.70 single). The short, blustery ferry ride from Lisbon to Cacilhas is great fun and grants wonderful views of the city. Cacilhas is little more than a bustling bus and ferry terminal, surrounded by lively stalls and cafés, though its blue and white church is pretty. From the ferry terminal, head west towards the bridge along the waterfront, past O Ponto Final restaurant, and it's around fifteen minutes' walk to the **Elevador Panorâmico da Boca do Vento** (daily 9.30am–6pm; €3 return; ☎212 900 071), a sleek lift that whisks you 30m up the cliff face to the attractive old part of Almada, giving fantastic views over the river and city.

On the heights above Almada stand the outstretched arms of **Cristo Rei**, a relatively modest version of Rio de Janeiro's Christ statue, built in 1959. A lift at the statue (daily: June–Sept 9am–7.30pm; Oct–May 9am–6pm; €1.50; bus #101 from outside the Cacilhas ferry terminal; ☎212 751 000) shuttles you a further 80m up to a dramatic viewing platform, from where, on a clear day, you can catch a glimpse of the glistening roof of the Pena palace at Sintra.

▼ CACILHAS FERRY

Caparica

Via Rapida express (hourly; 30 min) or slower local buses (every 15–30min; 50min), from Cacilhas or from Lisbon's Praça de Espanha (every 30–60min; 40min–60min).

Lisbon's main seaside resort, Caparica, was, according to legend, named after the find of a cloak (*capa*) full of golden coins. Today it is high-rise, tacky and packed at weekends in summer, but don't let that put you off. Its family atmosphere, restaurants and beachside cafés full of tanned surfers make it a thoroughly enjoyable day out.

From May to early October, buses stop at the bus park near the beginning of the sands. In winter, buses head straight to the station in Praça Padre Manuel Bernardes, in which case it's best to get off at the first stop in Caparica, on the edge of the tree-lined Praça da Liberdade, five minutes from the beach. From Praça da Liberdade the pedestrianized Rua dos Pescadores – lined with cafés, restaurants and inexpensive guesthouses – heads down to the seafront.

From the beach, a **narrow-gauge mini-railway** (May–Sept daily every 30min from 9am–7.30pm; €3.80 return, or €2.35 return for first nine stops) runs south along 8km or so of fantastic beach and dunes to **Fonte da Telha**, a

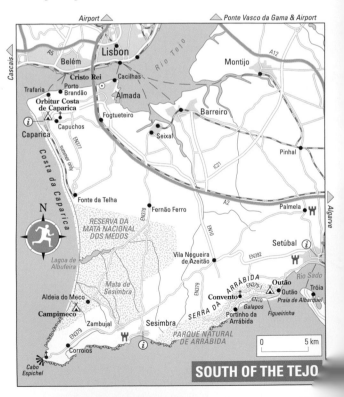

SOUTH OF THE TEJO

scattered resort of beach huts, cafés and restaurants. You can jump off at any one of the nineteen stops en route; earlier stops tend to be family-oriented, while later ones are, on the whole, younger, with nudity (though officially illegal) more or less the norm. This is especially true around stops 18 and 19, a predominately gay area.

Lagoa de Albufeira

Busy in summer with swimmers and windsurfers and at other times frequented by fishermen, the Lagoa de Albufeira is a lovely spot, though you'll need your own car to reach it as public transport is virtually non-existent. The lagoon is home to mallards, shovellers and woodcocks, and there's a superb neighbouring beach pummelled by surf.

Aldeia do Meco

Despite being swamped by a fair bit of development, the village of Aldeia do Meco is an attractive place, though again you'll need a car to get here. Its low cliff-backed beach, Praia do Meco, is popular with nudists; take care when swimming as the currents can be lethal. Like the other beaches on this coast, it is

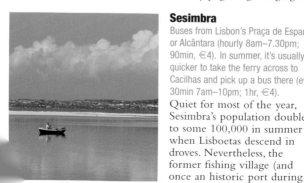

▲ PILGRIMAGE LODGINGS, CABO ESPICHEL

prone to overcrowding in July and August but can be almost deserted out of season.

Cabo Espichel

Buses from Sesimbra (2 daily at 1.30pm & 2.50pm, return at 2pm & 3.30pm). Wild and windswept cliffs drop almost vertically several hundred feet into the Atlantic at Cabo Espichel, an end-of-the-world plateau where the road stops at a church fronted by a wide square enclosed on three sides by ramshackle, arcaded eighteenth-century pilgrimage lodgings.

Sesimbra

Buses from Lisbon's Praça de Espanha or Alcântara (hourly 8am–7.30pm; 90min, €4). In summer, it's usually quicker to take the ferry across to Cacilhas and pick up a bus there (every 30min 7am–10pm; 1hr, €4). Quiet for most of the year, Sesimbra's population doubles to some 100,000 in summer when Lisboetas descend in droves. Nevertheless, the former fishing village (and once an historic port during

OA DE ALBUFEIRA

▲ PRAIA DO MECO

the times of the Discoveries) is still an admirable spot, with excellent swimming from the long beach and an endless row of café-restaurants. At night, families crowd the line of restaurants east of the fort, along Avenida 25 de Abril, and round the little Largo dos Bombaldes, with its warren of cobbled alleyways heading uphill.

Sesimbra's fishing port, Porto de Abrigo, is a pleasant ten-minute walk west along the sea front. As well as colourful fishing boats and the usual fishing activity, a variety of **boat trips** depart most days during the summer: the Clube Naval offers half-day cruises on a traditional sailing boat, the *Santiago* (details on Ⓦwww.naval-sesimbra.pt).

For panoramas over the surrounding countryside and coastline make the short drive (or a stiff half-hour climb from the centre) to the battlemented **Moorish castle** (open access; free) which sits on the heights above town. Within the walls are a café, pretty eighteenth-century church and cemetery.

Parque Natural da Arrábida

Surprisingly wild and unspoilt, the Parque Natural da Arrábida is just an hour's drive south of the capital. With a coastline sheltering some of Portugal's calmest sandy bays, the park spreads across a 500m-high granite ridge known as the Serra da Arrábida, visible for miles around and home to wildcats, badgers, polecats,

Mata de Sesimbra

The area north and west of Sesimbra, known as the Mata de Sesimbra, is being developed, in the words of the promoters, as the world's first "integrated sustainable building, tourism, nature conservation and reforestation programme". Partly funded by the World Wide Fund for Nature (WWF), all the buildings in the 8000-hectare site will be water and energy efficient and will eventually offer housing for up to 20,000 people, along with golf courses, three hotels and cinemas. Despite the scale of the project, only ten percent of the area will be built on, with much of the land set aside for reforestation, though it will not be completed for at least a decade. Details are available at Ⓦwww.oneplanetliving.org.

buzzards and Bonelli eagles. The most dramatic sections of the park are traversed by two roads, the twisting N379–1, which winds across its upper stretches, and the narrow EN10–4 coastal road. Note, however, that in July and August, an elaborate one-way system operates here to control the beach traffic, with the coast road operating westwards only until 7pm.

Apart from the views, the main highlight of the upper road is the **Convento da Arrábida** (Wed & Sun 3–4pm; advance booking required on ☏212 180 520), built by Franciscan monks in the sixteenth century. Dazzling white buildings tumble down a steep hillside, offering stunning ocean views.

Down on the coast road, the tiny harbour village of **Portinho da Arrábida** stands at one end of the region's best beaches – wonderful out of season, when it is often deserted. The port is guarded by a tiny seventeenth-century fort, now housing the interesting **Museu Oceanográfico** (Tues–Fri 10am–4pm, Sat 3–6pm, €2) displaying marine animals from the region – live in tanks, or stuffed and mounted.

Setúbal

Buses from Lisbon's Praça de Espanha (every 30min 7am–8pm; 1hr), and from Cacilhas (hourly 7am–midnight; 50min). The large, industrial port-town of Setúbal is the departure point for year-round **dolphin-watching trips** May–Sept daily 10am & ~m, Oct–April Sat & a only; minimum six le required; weather permitting; €30; ☏265 238 000, ⓦwww.vertigemazul .com), run by Vertigem Azul (Rua Praia da Saúde 11d). The Sado estuary and coast off Arrábida is one of the best places in Portugal to see bottle-nosed dolphins.

José Maria da Fonseca wine vaults and museum

Rua José Augusto Coelho, Vila Nogueira de Azeitão ☏212 198 940, ⓦwww.jmf. pt. Mon–Fri 9.30am–noon & 2.30–4.15pm, Sat & Sun 10am–noon & 2.30–4pm; free. Advance bookings essential. Buses from Lisbon's Praça de Espanha (hourly 8am–7.30pm; 45min). The big highlight in the otherwise dull town of Vila Nogueira de Azeitão is the José Maria da Fonseca wine vaults and museum. Forty-five-minute tours (available in English) take in the vaults, which are lined with a superb series of azulejos – some dating back to the fifteenth century – and provides an interesting introduction to the local wine, Setúbal Moscatel. The tours also include a free tasting.

▲ SURFING AT CAPARICA

Restaurants

O Barbas

Praia da Costa, Caparica ☎ 212 900
163. Mon, Tues & Thurs noon–2am.
With window seats looking out
over the sands and cafe seats on
the promenade, *O Barbas* (*The
Beard*) is an atmospheric beach
restaurant with affordable fish,
paella and *cataplanas* to die for.
You'll probably see the owner –
he's the one with the huge
amounts of facial hair. From
Rua das Pescadores, head north
up the esplanade; the restaurant
is on your right.

O Galeão

Portinho da Arrábida ☎ 212 180 533.
Mon & Wed–Sun noon–10pm.
Prominent seafront restaurant set
on stilts over the water, where
you can sit on a terrace and
look down on the fish before
tucking into their friends,
grilled or fried.

Cervejaria Farol

Alfredo Dinis Alex 1–3, Cacilhas ☎ 212
765 248. Tues & Thurs–Sun 9am–
midnight. The most high-profile
seafood restaurant in Cacilhas,
with fine views across the Tejo
to match. If you feel extravagant,
it's hard to beat the lobsters,
though other dishes are
moderately priced. Azulejos on
the wall show the old *farol*
(lighthouse) that once stood
here – the restaurant is located
along the quayside, on the right
as you leave the ferry.

Pedra Alta

Largo dos Bombaldes 13, Sesimbra
☎ 212 231 791. Daily noon–11pm.

▲ BARRELS FROM FONSECA WINE MUSEUM

Considering its prime position
on the seafront square, the well-
prepared seafood and fresh fish
are good value.

Bars

Sereia

Avda dos Náufragos 22, Sesimbra
☎ 934 547 758. Daily noon–midnight.
Lively café-bar with a young
crowd attracted by loud music, a
dartboard and outdoor tables
facing the sea.

Tarquinho Bar

Praia da Costa, Caparica ☎ 212 290
053. Daily 10am–midnight. A
popular surfers' hangout right
on the seafront promenade, with
cocktails, sangria and snacks
served at wooden outdoor tables
shaded by straw-mat roofs.
There are karaoke and Brazilian
theme nights too.

Accommodation

Hotels

Lisbon has no shortage of sumptuous **hotels** set in historic buildings and palaces, along with numerous less exclusive options in and around the centre. Besides hotels, there are **pensions** (*pensões;* singular *pensão*) and **guesthouses** (*residenciais;* singular *residencial*), officially graded from one to three stars, with the more basic ones having little more than a basin in the room, while three-star places usually include ensuite bathroom facilities, telephone and a TV.

Prices given below are for a one-night stay in the cheapest double room available in high season. Prices drop considerably out of season. All the pensions, guesthouses and hotels reviewed below have an ensuite bath or shower unless otherwise stated and include breakfast: anything from bread, jam and coffee to a generous spread of rolls, cereals, croissants, cold meat, cheese and fruit.

The Baixa

Hotel Duas Nações Rua da Vitória 41 ☎213 460 710, ✆www.duasnacoes .com. Classy, pleasantly faded nineteenth-century hotel with helpful, English-speaking reception staff. €30 for rooms with shared facilities; up to €55 for ensuite. Also has rooms for three to four people.

Residencial Insulana Rua da Assunção 52 ☎213 423 131, ✆wwwinsulana.cjb .net. Go upstairs past a series of shops to reach one of the more upmarket Baixa options. With its own bar overlooking a quiet pedestrianized street, the hotel's smart rooms are complete with satellite TV and a/c. English-speaking staff. €55.

Rossio and around

Hotel Avenida Palace Rua 1° de Dezembro 123 ☎213 218 100, ✆www.hotel -avenida-palace.pt. Built at the end of the nineteenth century, and rumoured to have a secret door direct to neighbouring Rossio station, this is one of Lisbon's most historic and grandest of hotels. Despite extensive modernization, the traditional feel has been maintained with stacks of chandeliers, period furniture, mirrors and marble throughout. There are 82 spacious rooms, each with high ceilings and colossal bathrooms. British artists Gilbert and George stay here on their frequent Lisbon visits. €260.

Hotel Lisboa Tejo Rua dos Condes de Monsanto 2 ☎218 866 182, ✆www .evidenciahoteis.com. This historic Baixa

Albergaria Senhora do Monte	16
As Janelas Verdes	48
Casa de São Mamede	17
Hotel Amazónia	9
Hotel Anjo Azul	36
Hotel Avenida Palace	29
Hotel Bairro Alto	44
Hotel Borges	40
Hotel Britania	10
Hotel Dom Carlos Parque	7
Hotel Duas Nações	39
Hotel Flamingo	8
Hotel Lisboa Plaza	15
Hotel Lisboa Regency Chiado	42
Hotel Lisboa Tejo	30
Hotel Metrópole	32
Hotel Miraparque	3
Hotel NH Liberdade	13
Hotel Portugal	27
Hotel Príncipe Real	20
Hotel Real Palácio	1
Hotel Suíço Atlântico	22
Hotel Veneza	11
Lapa Palace	46
Palácio Belmonte	37
Pensão Camões	34
Pensão Coimbra e Madrid	31
Pensão Gerês	24
Pensão Globo	26
Pensão Londres	23
Pensão Luar	35
Pensão Ninho das Águias	28
Pensão Portuense	19
Pensão Santa Catarina	43
Pensão São João da Praça & Sé Guest House	45
Pousada de Juventude de Lisboa	2
Residencial 13° de Sorte	14
Residencial Alegria	18
Residencial Avenida Alameda	4
Residencial Dom Sancho I	12
Residencial Florescente	21
Residencial Insulana	38
Residencial York House	47
Ritz Four Seasons	6
Sana Classic Rex Hotel	5
Solar do Castelo	33
Solar dos Mouros	41
VIP Eden	25

0   250 m

▽ Belém and Alcântara

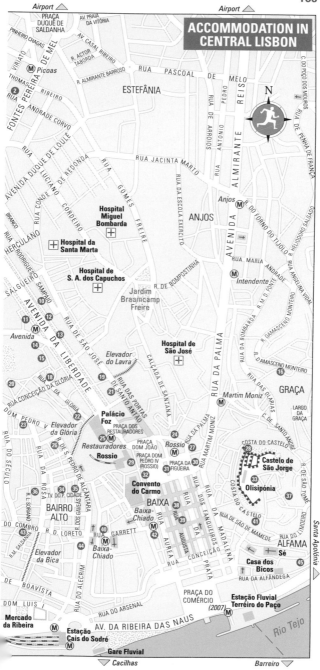

ACCOMMODATION IN CENTRAL LISBON

townhouse has been given a superb make-over, and now combines bare brickwork with cutting-edge design. Wood-floored rooms aren't huge but come with modems and minibars, and downstairs there is a boutiquey, Gaudí-inspired bar. €120.

Hotel Metrópole Rossio 30 ☎213 219 030, ⊛www.almeidahotels.com. Characterful early twentieth century three-star, with an airy lounge bar offering superb views over Rossio and the castle. The simply furnished but spacious rooms are comfortable, but the square can be quite noisy at night. €150.

Hotel Portugal Rua João das Regras 4 ☎218 877 581, ⊕218 867 343. Amazing century-old two-star that has suffered an appalling conversion, with its high decorative ceilings chopped up by wall partitions. Nevertheless, the rooms are comfortable and air-conditioned, the bathrooms are lined with marble and there's an ornate TV room with period furniture. €70.

Hotel Suíço Atlântico Rua da Glória 3 ☎213 461 713, ✉h.suisso.atlantico @grupofbarata.com. Popular mid-range hotel in a good location, close to the *elevador* to Bairro Alto. Rooms are fairly standard, though some come with balconies looking down on to seedy Rua da Glória. The mock-baronial bar and bright breakfast room are the highlights. €55.

Pensão Coimbra e Madrid Praça da figueira 3–3° ☎213 424 808, ⊕213 423 264. Best budget choice on the square is this large, decently run (if faintly shabby) *pensão*, with superb views of Rossio, Praça da figueira and the castle beyond. In so central a position, the front-facing rooms inevitably suffer from noise. No breakfast, but *Pastelaria Suíça* is right underneath. €35.

Pensão Portuense Rua das Portas de Santo Antão 151–153 ☎213 461 749, ⊛www.pensaoportuense.com. Singles, doubles and rooms for up to four in a family-run place that takes good care of its guests. The spacious bathrooms are kept meticulously clean, and breakfast includes fresh bread and preserves. €52.

Pensão Gerês Calçada da Garcia 6 ☎218 810 497, ⊛www.pensaogeres .com. Set on a steep side street just off Rossio, the beautiful, tiled entrance hall and chunky wooden doors set the tone for one of the more characterful central options. The simple rooms of varying sizes are minimally furnished, though all have TV and bathroom. Internet access on request; no breakfast. €65.

Residencial Florescente Rua das Portas de Santo Antão 99 ☎213 426 609, ⊛www.residencialflorescente. com. This is the best guesthouse on this pedestrianized street. There's a large selection of air-conditioned rooms across four floors (some with TV and small bathroom), so if you don't like the look of the room you're shown – and some are very cramped – ask about alternatives. Be warned that street-facing rooms can be noisy. There is also a lounge and Internet access for a small fee. €70.

VIP Eden Praça dos Restauradores 18–24 ☎213 216 600, ⊛www .viphotels.com. Compact studios and apartments sleeping up to four people are available within the impressively converted Eden cinema. They are somewhat cheaply furnished, but get a ninth-floor apartment with a balcony and you'll have the best views and be just below the superb breakfast bar and rooftop pool. All studios come with dishwashers, microwaves and satellite TV. Disabled access. €125 for studios and double apartments, €180 for larger apartments.

Addresses

Addresses are written in the form "Rua do Crucifixo 50–4°", meaning the fourth storey of no. 50, Rua do Crucifixo. The addition of e, d or r/c at the end means the entrance is on the left (*esquerda*), right (*direita*) or on the ground floor (*rés-do-chão*). Don't be unduly put off by some fairly insalubrious staircases, but do be aware that rooms facing onto the street can often be unbearably noisy.

The Alfama

Pensão São João da Praça Rua de São João da Praça 97–2° ⓣ218 862 591, ⓕ218 881 378. Attractive town house with street-facing wrought-iron balconies, though the rooms are slightly shabby. It's a quiet and friendly, if simple, establishment with a range of rooms, from €35 with shared bathroom, up to €55 with bath (all rates include breakfast).

Sé Guest House Rua de São João da Praça 97–1° ⓣ218 864 400, ⓕ263 271 612. Characterfully done-up nineteenth-century town house with wooden floors, African artefacts and bright, airy rooms with TVs and minibars. Despite the communal bathrooms, it has a more upmarket feel than the *Pensão São João da Praça* in the same building. €70.

Castelo, Mouraria and Graça

Albergaria Senhora do Monte Calçada do Monte 39 ⓣ218 866 002, ⓔsenhoradomonte@hotmail.com. Head north from Largo da Graça, taking the first left into Rua Damasceno Monteiro – Calçada do Monte is the first right. Comfortable, modern hotel in a sublime location with views of the castle and Graça convent from the south-facing rooms, some of which have terraces. Breakfast is taken on the fourth-floor terrace, and private parking is available. €100.

Palácio Belmonte Pateo Dom Fradique 14 ⓣ218 816 600, ⓦwww .palaciobelmonte.com. If you have over €500 a night to burn for a special occasion, check availability at this private club which rents out rooms. A highly atmospheric fifteenth-century palace, the property retains much of its original decor apart from the odd designer bathroom. There are fabulous eighteenth-century azulejos, soaring ceilings and wood floors throughout, along with six individual suites, including one set in a tower with a 360-degree view of Alfama. There's also a small garden with plunge pool and terrace. Upwards of €500.

Pensão Ninho das Águias Costa do Castelo 74 ⓣ218 854 070. Superbly sited its own view-laden terrace-garden, on the street looping around and below the castle, this is justifiably one of the most popular budget places in the city. Climb up the staircase and past the birdcages. Rooms are spartan but bright, though avoid the dingy basement room. Book in advance as there are only sixteen rooms. €45 for shared facilities, otherwise €50. No breakfast.

Solar do Castelo Rua das Cozinhas 2 ⓣ218 870 909, ⓦwww.heritage.pt. A tastefully renovated eighteenth-century mansion abutting the castle walls on the site of the former palace kitchens, parts of which remain. Its fourteen rooms cluster found a tranquil inner courtyard, where you can enjoy a vast buffet breakfast. It's not cheap and rooms aren't enormous, but most boast balconies overlooking the castle grounds, and service is second to none. €245.

Solar dos Mouros Rua do Milagre de Santo António 6 ⓣ218 854 940, ⓦwww .solardosmouros.com. A tall Alfama town house done out in a contemporary style with its own bar. Each of the twelve rooms offers fantastic vistas of the river or castle and comes with CD player and a/c. There's plenty of modern art to enjoy if you tire of the view. €240.

Cais do Sodré and Chiado

Hotel Bairro Alto Praça Luís de Camões 8 ⓣ213 408 223, ⓦwww .bairroaltohotel.com. A grand eighteenth-century building that has been modernized into a fashionable boutique hotel. Rooms and communal areas still have a period feel – the lift takes a deep breath before rattling up its six floors – but modern touches appear in the form of DVDs in rooms, a rooftop café and swish split-level bar full of comfy cushions. €280.

Hotel Borges Rua Garrett 108 ⓣ213 461 951, ⓦwww.lisbonhotelborges .com. In a prime spot on Chiado's main street, this traditional and elegantly furnished three-star is very popular, though front rooms can be noisy. Double or triple rooms are plain and rather small but are good value. €65.

Hotel Lisboa Regency Chiado Rua Nova do Almada 114 ☏213 256 100, ⊛www .regency-hotels-resorts.com. for style and modern flair it would be hard to find a better central hotel. Designed by Álvaro Siza Viera – the architect responsible for the Chiado redevelopment – and with Oriental-inspired interior decor by the highly rated Portuguese designer Pedro Espírito Santo, the Lisboa Regency is spacious and uncluttered. Orange segment-shaped windows give glimpses of Chiado in one direction and the whole city in the other. The cheapest rooms lack much of an outlook, but the best ones have terraces with stunning views towards the castle – a view you get from the bar terrace too. All rooms have modems. Limited parking available. €195.

Pensão Santa Catarina Rua Dr Luís de Almeida e Albuquerque 6 ☏213 466 106. On a quiet side street near the popular Miradouro de Santa Catarina, this simple little guest house has decent rooms and friendly owners. €48.

The Bairro Alto

Hotel Anjo Azul Rua Luz Soriano 75 ☏213 478 069, ⊛www.anjoazul .cb2web.com. The city's first gay hotel, the "Blue Angel" is set in a lovely blue-tiled eighteenth-century town house right in the heart of the area's nightlife. There are twenty simple but attractive rooms set over four floors (€50), some with ensuite facilities (€60). No breakfast, however there is a communal kitchen.

Pensão Camões Trav. do Poço da Cidade 38–1° ☏213 467 510, ☏213 464 048. Small rooms, the best with balconies (others are somewhat gloomy), in the Bairro Alto grid – so expect lots of noise, especially at weekends. A superb breakfast is provided (April–Oct only) in a pleasant dining room, and the English-speaking owners are very friendly. €45, or €35 with shared bath.

Pensão Globo Rua do Teixeira 37 ☏213 462 279 w⊛www.pensaoglobo.com. Attractive house on a relatively quiet street, bang in the middle of the Bairro Alto. fifteen varied rooms: all are simple and most are reasonably large with TVs, though avoid those without windows. There's a bar downstairs. No breakfast. €30.

Pensão Luar Rua das Gáveas 101–1° ☏213 460 949 w⊛www.pensaoluar.com. Polished interior and decently furnished rooms (with shower and TV) varying in size, so ask to see first. Don't expect a quiet night as this is surrounded by bars and restaurants. No breakfast. €40.

Praça Princípe Real and around

Casa de São Mamede Rua da Escola Politécnica 159 ☏213 963 166, ☏213 951 896. On a busy street north of Praça do Prinçipe Real, this is a superb seventeenth-century town house with period fittings, bright breakfast room and a grand stained-glass window. Rooms are rather ordinary, but all are equipped with a TV. €75.

Hotel Princípe Real Rua da Alegria 53 ☏213 407 350, ⊛.www.hotel principereal.com. Recently renovated, this small four-star sits on a quiet street just below the Bairro Alto. Eighteen rooms, each with modern decor and some with balconies and superb city views. Best of all is the top-floor suite with stunning vistas (€155); other rooms €105.

Pensão Londres Rua Dom Pedro V 53 ☏213 462 203, ⊛.www.pensaolondres .com.pt. Wonderful old building with high ceilings and forty pleasant enough rooms spread across four floors, sleeping up to four. Some with tiny bathrooms (€70), those without are cheaper (€65), and the best ones have great views over the city. It has a reputation as a gay-friendly hotel, though not exclusively so.

São Bento, Santos, Estrela and Lapa

As Janelas Verdes Rua das Janelas Verdes 47 ☏213 218 200, ⊛www .heritage.pt. Highly recommended, this discreet, eighteenth-century town house, where Eça de Queirós was inspired to write *Os Maios*, is just metres from the Museu de Arte Antiga. Spacious rooms come with marble bathrooms, period furnishings and pictures, and breakfast is served in the delightful walled garden. The top-floor library and terrace command spectacular river views. Advance booking recommended. €235.

Lapa Palace Rua do Pau da Bandeira 4 ☏213 949 494, ⊛www.lapapalace.com. A stunning nineteenth-century mansion set in its own lush gardens, with dramatic vistas over the Tejo. Rooms are luxurious, and those in the Palace Wing are each decorated in a different style, from Classical to Art Deco. In the summer, barbecues are served by the outdoor pool. There's also a health club, disabled access and a list of facilities as long as your arm, from babysitting to banqueting. €430.

Residencial York House Rua das Janelas Verdes 32 ☏213 962 435, ⊛www .yorkhouselisboa.com. Located in a sixteenth-century Carmelite convent (and hidden from the main street by high walls), rooms here come with rugs, tiles and four-poster beds. The best are grouped around a beautiful interior courtyard, where drinks and meals are served in summer, and there's a highly rated restaurant. Advance bookings recommended. €150.

Alcântara and the docks

Pestana Palace Hotel Rua Jau 54 ☏213 615 600, ⊛www.pestana.com. Set in an early twentieth-century palace full of priceless works of art, most rooms at this five-star hotel are in tasteful modern wings that stretch either side of UNESCO World Heritage gardens. Most rooms have large terraces and lie a short walk from a sushi bar, a sunken outdoor pool with a fountain to swim out to, and an indoor pool and health club. The price, which can be greatly reduced for summer offers, includes a vast breakfast in the former ballroom. €430.

Avenida da Liberdade and around

Hotel Amazónia Trav. Fábrica dos Pentes ☏213 877 006, ⊛www .amazoniahotels.com. This spacious and modern three-star is in a quiet part of town and has a small outdoor pool. Top floor rooms come with city views, some with balconies. All rooms have satellite TVs and minibars. There's a downstairs bar and restaurant, car parking and disabled access. Good value. €120.

Hotel Britania Rua Rodrigues Sampaio 17 ☏213 155 016, ⊛www.heritage .pt. Designed in the 1940s by influential architect Cassiano Branco, this is a characterful Art Deco gem with huge airy rooms, each with traditional cork flooring and marble-clad bathrooms. The hotel interior, with library and bar, has been declared of national architectural importance. A somewhat ratty breakfast is charged as an extra. €164.

Hotel Dom Carlos Parque Avda Duque de Loulé 121 ☏213 512 590, ⊛www .domcarloshoteis.com. Decent three-star just off Praça Marquês de Pombal, with fair-sized rooms over eight floors, each with cable TV and videos. Some overlook the neighbouring police and fire stations, which can add to the noise. There's a downstairs bar with plasma TV and garage parking. €120.

Hotel Flamingo Rua Castilho 41 ☏213 841 200, ⊛www.bestwestern.com. Friendly, slightly faded three-star, but with an appealing atmosphere. Small rooms have cable TV and minibars. The downstairs bar, with its own pool table, looks like something out of *Cheers*. €85.

Hotel Lisboa Plaza Trav. Salitre 7 ☏213 218 200, ⊛www.heritage.pt. Just off Avenida da Liberdade, this bright, polished, four-star hotel is a real treat – dried flowers everywhere, marble bathrooms, bar, restaurant and views of the botanical garden from the rear rooms. Limited disabled access. Recommended. €156.

Hotel NH Liberdade Avenida da Liberdade 180B ☏213 514 060, ⊛www .nh-hotels.com. Discreetly tucked into the back of the Tivoli forum shopping centre off the main Avenida, this Spanish chain hotel offers ten floors of modern flair. The best rooms have balconies facing the traditional Lisbon houses at the back. Unusually for central Lisbon, there's a rooftop pool. There's also a bar and restaurant. €185, with special weekend rates at substantial reductions.

Hotel Veneza Avda da Liberdade 189 ☎213 522 618, ⒲www.3khoteis.com. Built in 1886, the distinguishing feature of this former town house is an ornate staircase, now flanked by modern murals of Lisbon. The smallish rooms are less individually styled, with bland furnishings. Buffet breakfast charged as an extra. Disabled access. €70.

Residencial Alegria Praça da Alegria 12 ☎213 220 670, ⒲www.alegrianet.com. friendly place in a great position, facing the leafy Praça da Alegria ("Happy Square"). Spacious, spotless rooms with TV, though front ones can be noisy. €50.

Residencial Dom Sancho I Avda da Liberdade 202–2° ☎213 513 160, ⒲www.domsancho.com. One of the few inexpensive options right on the avenue and, what's more, set in a grand old mansion with high ceilings and decorative cornices – though, as you'd expect, the front rooms are noisy. The large, air-conditioned rooms come with satellite TV. €80.

Residencial Treze da Sorte Rua do Salitre 13 ☎213 531 851, ⒲www .trezedasorte.no.sapo.pt. Its name translates roughly as "Lucky 13" and the owners are indeed fortunate with this well-run and good-value guesthouse set in a tall, traditional building. Spacious rooms are spread across five floors, each with cable TV and fridge; breakfast not included. €55.

Parque Eduardo VII and the Gulbenkian

Hotel Miraparque Avda Sidónio Pais 12 ☎213 524 286, ⒠miraparque @esoterica.pt. Housed in an attractive building overlooking Parque Eduardo VII, the Miraparque is pleasantly old-fashioned, though the reception staff can be a bit brusque. All rooms come with TV, and there's a decent bar and restaurant. €95.

Hotel Real Palácio Rua Tomás Ribeiro 115 ☎213 199 500, ⒲www.hoteisreal .com. Though most of the rooms are in a bland modern extension, the best ones here are in the original seventeenth-century palace, with its own courtyard, now housing a café-bar. five-star facilities include a health club and restaurant. €200.

Residencial Avenida Alameda Avda Sidónio Pais 4 ☎213 532 186, ⒠213 526 703. Very pleasant three-star *residencial* with air-conditioned rooms, all with park views, on a quiet side road. €60.

Ritz Four Seasons Rua Rodrigo da Fonseca 88 ☎213 811 400, ⒲www .fourseasons.com. This vast building is one of the grandest – and most expensive – hotels in the city, with huge, airy rooms, terraces overlooking the park, and public areas replete with marble, antiques, original artwork and overly attentive staff. There's also a fitness centre, spa and highly rated restaurant. Disabled access. €340.

Sana Classic Rex Hotel Rua Castilho 169 ☎213 882 161, ⒲www.sanahotels .com. One of the less outrageously priced hotels in this neck of the woods – look out for special deals on its website – with an in-house restaurant and small but well-equipped rooms. The best are at the front, sporting large balconies overlooking Parque Eduardo VII. €150.

Sintra

See map on p.143

Lawrence's Hotel Rua Consigliéri Pedroso 38–40, Sintra-Vila ☎219 105 500, ⒲lawrenceshotel.com. This professes to be the oldest hotel in Portugal, dating from 1764 (and claiming a visit from Byron) but reopened as a five-star under Dutch ownership in 1999. Book ahead for one of eleven large rooms and five suites, all elegantly furnished. There are plenty of comfortable communal areas, including a highly rated restaurant which serves upmarket Portuguese cuisine. The hotel can also organize golfing packages. €240.

Palácio de Seteais Rua Barbosa du Bocage 8 ☎219 233 200, ⒲www .tivolihotels.com. The "Seven Sighs", one of the most sophisticated palaces in Portugal, is on the Monserrate road, a few minutes' drive from the centre of Sintra-Vila. Completed in the last years of the eighteenth century and maintained today as an immensely luxurious hotel, it even boasts a majestic Neoclassical arch. The large rooms have period furniture and very comfy beds – they're popular with honeymooners.

– while the landscaped garden has its own superb swimming pool. €200.

Pensão Nova Sintra Largo Afonso d'Albuquerque 25, Estefânia ☎219 230 220, ⓦwww.novasintra.com. Very smart *pensão* in a big mansion, whose elevated terrace-café overlooks a busy street. The modern rooms all have cable TV and shiny marble floors, and there's a decent restaurant downstairs. €75.

Piela's Avda Desiderio Cambournac 1–3, Estefânia ☎219 241 691. Popular budget accommodation in a swish, renovated town house above a cybercafé, on a busy road. The welcoming English-speaking proprietor offers rooms of varying sizes, each with TV, from €50. Triples also available. No breakfast.

Residencial Sintra Trav. dos Alvares, São Pedro ☎ & ⓕ219 230 738, ⓔpensao .residencial.sintra@clix.pt. The best mid-range option in the area, this rambling old *pensão* has soaring ceilings, wooden floors and oodles of character. There's a substantial garden with a swimming pool and the giant rooms can easily accommodate extra beds – so it's great for families. You'll need to book ahead in summer; in winter there's a log fire in the communal lounge. €100.

The Sintra coast and Queluz

Hotel Arribas Praia Grande ☎219 289 050, ⓦwww.hotelarribas.com. This modern three-star hotel is plonked ungraciously at the north end of the beach, the only building right on the sands. Rooms are enormous and come with minibars and satellite TV – those with a sea view are hard to fault. There are also sea-water swimming pools, a restaurant and café terrace. Also has family rooms sleeping up to four. Disabled access. €115.

Pousada Dona Maria I Largo do Palácio, Palácio de Queluz, Queluz ☎214 356 158, ⓦwww.pousadas.pt. The pink-faced *pousada* (inn), with its distinctive clock tower, gives you the chance to stay in an annexe of one of Lisbon's grandest palaces. Though once used as the palace staff quarters, these days the huge rooms are lavishly

furnished, with ornate drapes and big comfy chairs. Disabled access. €205.

São Saturnia Azóia ☎219 283 192, ⓦwww.saosat.com. Reached down a steep track – look for the sign left just past the turning to Cabo da Roca, before Azóia – this former convent dates back to the twelfth century and sits in a valley where time seems to stand still. The six rooms, three suites and self-catering apartments are all traditionally furnished while the rambling communal areas are all weathered beams, bare bricks and low ceilings. There's a small outdoor pool, barbecue area, geese, cats, and lots of terraces with stunning views – truly magical. €160.

Cascais coast

See map on p.156

Farol Design Hotel Avda Rei Humberto II de Italia, Cascais ☎214 823 490, ⓦwww.cascais.org. Right on the seafront, this is an ideal option if you like both traditional and contemporary architecture. A new designer wing has been welded onto a sixteenth-century villa, and the decor combines wood and marble with modern steel and glass. The best rooms have sea views and terraces, and there's also a bar, restaurant and outdoor pool facing a fine rocky foreshore. Staff wear alarming, surgeon-like uniforms. €215, or €260 with sea views.

Hotel Albatroz Rua Frederico Arouca 100, Cascais ☎214 847 380, ⓦwww .albatrozhotels.com. Built in the nineteenth century as a royal retreat, seaside hotels don't come much grander than this – one of the best in the region, with glorious views from some rooms (for which you pay extra) and top-of-the-range facilities. There's a lovely swimming pool on the ocean terrace, and a restaurant. €240, up to €325 with sea views.

Hotel Baía Avda C. Grande Guerra, Cascais ☎214 831 033, ⓕ214 831 095, ⓦwww.hotelbaia.com. Large seafront hotel boasting 113 rooms with a/c and satellite TV; front ones have balconies overlooking the beach. There's a great rooftop terrace complete with a covered pool, and a good restaurant. Parking at €10 a day. €125.

Solar Dom Carlos Rua Latino Coelho 8, Cascais ☎214 828 115, ⓦwww .solardomcarlos.com. The best value place in town, set in a sixteenth-century mansion on a quiet backstreet in the pretty western side of Cascais. Dom Carlos once stayed here, hence the royal chapel, which still survives. The tiled interior stays cool in summer, there's a garden and car parking, while attractive rooms come with satellite TV and fridge. €60.

Hotel Cascais Mirage Avenida Marginal 8554 ☎210 060 619, ⓦwww .cascaismirage.com. This ultra-modern five-star has won design awards – its stepped, glass-fronted nine floors are built into the slope behind it, while inside, the huge lobby and communal areas are bathed in light. Rooms are gigantic and all have sea-facing balconies, and there's a pool, restaurant and crisp, friendly service. Parking. €290.

South of the Tejo

Pensão Real Rua Mestre Manuel 18, Caparica ☎212 918 870, ⓦwww .hotel-real.com. friendly and reasonable central *pensão*, a few minutes' walk from the beach, just off Rua dos Pescadores. Small but pleasant rooms come with TV and bath and some have balconies and sea views. €80.

Sana Park Avda 25 de Abril, Sesimbra ☎212 289 000, ⓦwww.sanahotels.com. The best upmarket choice in Sesimbra, right on the seafront. The plush rooms have satellite TVs and minibars, and there's a sauna and pool (open to non-guests), a restaurant and groovy rooftop bar. €135, or €166 for sea views.

Hostels

The central **booking office** for Portugal's youth hostels (*pousadas de juventude*) is Movijovem, near metro Saldanha at Avda Duque de Ávila 137 (☎217 232 100/707 203 030, ⓦwww .pousadas.juventude.pt). A youth hostel card is required for all Portuguese hostels, but if you don't have one you can buy one on your first night's stay. Unless stated, prices do not include breakfast.

Pousada de Juventude de Catalazete Estrada Marginal, Oeiras ☎214 430 638, ⓔcatalazete@movijovem.pt. Take bus #44 from the airport. This hostel is set in an eighteenth-century sea-fort overlooking the sea pools in Oeiras, a beach suburb on the train line to Cascais. Reception is open 8am to midnight. With four- or six-bedded dorms (€13) and simple twin rooms from €28 (or €36 ensuite). Parking.

Lisboa Parque das Nações Rua de Moscavide 47–101, Parque das Nações ☎218 920 890, ⓔliboaparque @movijovem.pt. Map p.137. About five minutes' walk northeast of the Torre Vasco da Gama, towards the bridge, this smart, modern youth hostel has a pool table and disabled access. There are ten double rooms at €36 per room and eighteen four-bedded dorms at €13 per person. Disabled access.

Pousada de Juventude da Almada Quinta do Bucelinho, Pragal, Almada ☎212 943 491, ⓔalmada@movijovem .pt. On the south side of the Tejo – with terrific views back over Lisbon – this is not particularly convenient for sightseeing in the city, but is within striking distance of the Caparica beaches and Cacilhas. It has a games room, disabled access and Internet facilities. Over twenty four-bedded dorms at €16 per person, and thirteen twin-bedded rooms with their own toilet at €36 per room; also apartments for €70.

Pousada de Juventude de Lisboa Rua Andrade Corvo 46 ☎213 532 696, ⓔlisboa@movijovem.pt. Map pp.168–169. This is the main city hostel, set in a rambling old building by metro Picoas, with a small bar (open 6pm to midnight), canteen (reserve meals in advance; served 1–2pm & 7–8pm), TV room and disabled access. Thirty rooms sleeping four or six people (with shared bathrooms) for €16 per person; or doubles with private shower for €43 per room. The price includes breakfast.

Pousada de Juventude de Setúbal Largo José Afonso, Setúbal ☎265 534 431, ✉setubal@movijovem.pt. Map p.160. An all-glass fronted modern hostel right in the middle of one of Setúbal's main squares, close to the docks. Six four-bedded rooms from €5 per person, four doubles with bath from €15 or €12 for doubles without bath.

Campsites

There are some decent campsites within commuting distance of Lisbon, including near the Atlantic beaches of Costa da Caparica, Guincho and south of the Tejo. Expect to pay around €5 per person (half-price for children) and from €8 per tent in high season. The Portuguese camping organization is **Orbitur** (🌐www.orbitur.pt). Members get a ten percent discount at their campsites in the Lisbon region. Check out 🌐www.roteiro-campista.pt for details of other campsites.

Campimeco Praia das Bicas, 2km north-west of Aldeio do Meco ☎212 683 394, ☎212 683 844. Map p.160. Upmarket campsite, a short walk from Praia das Bicas, with tennis courts, restaurant, pool and mini-market.

Orbitur Costa de Caparica Avda Afonso de Albuquerque, Quinta de St António, Monte de Caparica ☎212 901 366, ✉info@orbitur.pt. Map p.160. One of the few campsites in Caparica open to

non-members, with good facilities including tennis courts and a mini-market, but it's not for those looking for solitude.

Orbitur Guincho Lugar da Areia, Guincho ☎214 870 450, ✉info@orbitur.pt. Close to Guincho beach among the pine trees, and served by bus from Cascais. It has tennis courts, mini-market and café, with bungalows and caravans for rent too.

Outão Estrada da Figueirinha, Praia de Albarquel ☎265 238 318. Map p.160. Simple campsite set amongst trees, close to the small Praia de Albarquel, 5km east of Pontinho da Arrábida.

Parque Municipal de Campismo Estrada da Circunvalação, Parque Florestal de Monsanto ☎217 623 105, ☎217 623 106. The main city campsite is very well-equipped, complete with bungalows, a swimming pool and shops. However, it is a 6km trek west of the centre, with the entrance on the park's west side – take bus #43 from Praça da figueira via Belém. Take care in the park after dark, though the campsite itself is secure.

Essentials

Arrival

However you arrive, it is easy to get to central Lisbon. The airport is right on the edge of the city and is well served by buses and taxis. The city's train stations are all centrally located with direct access to the metro; the two main bus stations are also close to metro stops.

By air

The aeroporto da Portela (☎218 413 700, ⓦ www.ana-aeroporto.pt) is just twenty minutes north of the city centre and has a tourist office (daily 7am–midnight, ☎218 450 660), a 24hr exchange bureau, currency exchange machines, ATMs and left-luggage facilities.

The easiest way to get into the centre is by **taxi**; a journey to Rossio should cost €10–13. Prepaid taxi vouchers are also available from the tourist office but, apart from helping you to queue-jump, don't work out any cheaper.

Alternatively, catch the #91 **Aerobus** (☎966 298 558) which departs every twenty minutes (daily 7.45am–8.45pm) from outside the terminal, and runs to Praça do Marquês de Pombal, Praça dos Restauradores, Rossio, Praça do Comércio and Cais do Sodré train station. Rides are free for TAP Air Portugal passengers (just show your boarding card). Otherwise on-board tickets also give you one day's travel on the city's buses and trams for €3. Local buses (#44 or #45) leave from outside the terminal to Praça dos Restauradores and Cais do Sodré station (every 10–15min, €1.20), though these are less convenient if you have a lot of luggage.

Direct buses to Estoril and Cascais (journey time 30–40min) depart from the airport hourly (on the hour from 7am, last departure 10.30pm, ⓦ www. scotturb .com).

By road and rail

Long-distance trains are run by CP (fare and timetable information on ☎808 208 208, ⓦ www.cp.pt). You'll arrive at Santa Apolónia station (see p.79), which is on the Gaivota metro line (from 2007); or else take bus #9, #39, #46 or #90 to Praça dos Restauradores or Rossio from outside the station. Most trains also call at Oriente station at Parque das Nações, which is on the red Oriente metro line. This station is more convenient for the airport or for the north and east of Lisbon.

The main national **bus** carrier is Rede Expressos (☎707 223 344, ⓦ www .rede-expressos.pt). Most services terminate at the main **bus station** at Sete Rios, next to the Jardim Zoológico metro line (for the centre) and Sete Rios train line (for Sintra and the northern suburbs). Many bus services also stop at the Oriente station at Parque das Nações, which is on the Oriente metro line.

Apart from Saturday afternoons and Sundays, when the city is quiet, **driving** round Lisbon is best avoided, though it is useful to hire a car to see the outlying sights (see p.188 for car rental companies).

Parking is very difficult in central Lisbon. Pay-and-display spots get snapped

---

Fly Less – Stay Longer!

Rough Guides believes in the good that travel does, but we are deeply aware of the impact of fuel emissions on climate change. We recommend taking fewer trips and staying for longer. If you can avoid travelling by air, please use an alternative, especially for journeys of under 1000km/600miles. And always offset your travel at ⓦ www.roughguides.com/climatechange.

up quickly and some of the local unemployed get by on tips for guiding drivers into empty spots; scratches have been known to appear suddenly on cars whose drivers do not leave tips, so you'd be better off heading for an official car park, for which you can expect to pay around €10 per day. Wherever you park, do not leave valuables inside: the break-in rate in the city centre is extremely high.

Information

The Portuguese Tourist Office is in Praça dos Restauradores (daily 9am–8pm; ☎213 463 314, ⓦwww. portugalinsite . pt), and is useful for general information. However, far more helpful is the **Lisbon Welcome Centre** at Rua do Arsenal 15, by Praça do Comércio, near the riverfront (see map on p.52; daily 9am–8pm; ☎210 312 810, ⓦwww.visitlisboa.com /atl-turismolisboa.pt), which can supply accommodation lists, bus timetables and maps.

Tourist offices at the airport (see p.181) and at Santa Apolónia station (Wed–Sat 8am–1pm, ☎218 821 606) can help you find accommodation, as can a few smaller "Ask Me" kiosks dotted around town, like the ones on Rua Augusta, and opposite Belém's Mosteiro dos Jerónimos). A free telephone information line dispenses basic information in English (Mon–Sat 9am–midnight, Sun 9am–8pm, ☎800 296 296).

There are also tourist offices in all the main day-trip destinations, with details as follows: Sintra Turismo (see map, p.143; daily 9am–7pm; ☎219 231 157, ⓦwww.cm-sintra.pt); Estoril Turismo (opposite the train station; daily; ☎214 663 813, ⓦwww.estorilcoast .com); Cascais Turismo (see map, p.156; daily; ☎214 868 204); Caparica Turismo (Avda da Liberdade 18, just off the main square; closed Mon–Fri 1–2pm, Sat afternoon and Sun; ☎212 900 071); and Sesimbra Turismo (Avda dos Náufragos, on the seafront; daily; ☎212 288 540).

Our **maps** will guide you around the city; Michelin's *Lisboa Planta Roteiro*, available in most good Lisbon bookshops, is the closest you'll find to an A–Z of the city.

The best **listings** magazine is *Agenda Cultural*, a free monthly produced by the town hall, which details current exhibitions and shows (in Portuguese). *Follow me Lisboa* is a watered-down English-language version produced by the local tourist office. All publications are available from the tourist offices and larger hotels. For **exhibitions** and **concerts**, pick up a schedule of events from the reception desks at the Gulbenkian Foundation (see p.127) or the Cultural Centre in Belém (see p.116).

City transport

Central Lisbon is compact enough to explore on foot, but don't be fooled by the apparent closeness of sights and streets as they appear on two-dimensional maps. There are some very steep hills to negotiate, although the city's quirky **elevadores** (funicular railways) will save you the steepest climbs around the Bairro Alto and Avenida da Liberdade. Elsewhere Lisbon's **Trams** (*electricos*) ply the narrow streets around the Alfama and beyond. They're hardly the fastest form of transport (the modern tram to Belém being the exception) but, along with the *elevadores*,

Useful bus routes

#1 Cais do Sodré to Charneca via the Baixa, Avda da Liberdade, Picoas (for the youth hostel) and Campo (for the bull ring).

#27 Marquês de Pombal to Belém via Estrela, Lapa and Alcântara.

#37 Praça da Figueira to Castelo de São Jorge via the Sé and Alfama.

#44/45 Outside the airport to Cais do Sodré via Marquês de Pombal, Avda da Liberdade and the Baixa.

#46 Santa Apolónia station to near Palácio dos Marquêses de Fronteira via Praça do Comércio, the Baixa, Avda da Liberdade, Praça Marquês de Pombal and the Fundação Gulbenkian.

#201 Night bus from Cais do Sodré to Belém via the docks; runs until 5am.

they are undoubtedly the most fun way to get around. Tram, bus and *elevador* stops are indicated by a sign marked "paragem", which carries route details.

The most efficient way to get around, however, is on the **metro**, with stations located close to most of the main sights. Suburban trains run from Rossio and Sete Rios stations out to Sintra and Queluz and from Cais do Sodré station to Belém, Estoril and Cascais, while ferries (☎218 820 348, ⓦ www.transtejo .pt) – worth taking for the terrific views of Lisbon alone – link Lisbon's Cais do Sodré to Cacilhas, with bus connections to the beach resort of Caparica.

Tickets and travel passes

It's possible just to buy a ticket each time you ride, but tickets bought in advance or a travel pass can save you money.

The best-value pass is the one-day **Bilhete Turístico** (€2.85), which allows unlimited travel on buses, trams, the metro and *elevadores* until midnight of the same day. It is obtainable from the kiosk above the entrance to the Elevador Santa Justa, in Praça da Figueira, and inside Restauradores metro station, among other places. For longer stays, you can buy a **Sete Colinas** card (€0.50), which you can load with a five-day pass (*bilhete cinco dias*, €13), also valid on all forms of city transport.

If you're planning some intensive sightseeing, the **Cartão Lisboa** (€13.50 for one day, €23 for two days, or €28 for three days) is a good buy. The card entitles you to unlimited rides on buses, trams, *elevadores* and the metro as well as entry to or discounts on around 25 museums. It's available from all the main tourist offices, including the one in the airport.

The metro

Lisbon's efficient metro – the *Metropolitano* – (daily 6.30am–1am; ☎213 558 457, ⓦ www.metrolisboa .pt; see map on backflap) is the best way of reaching the city's main sights, with trains every few minutes. Tickets cost €1.10 per journey, or €6.50 for a ten-ticket *caderneta* – sold at all stations. If you think you're going to use the metro a lot, buy a pass (see above).

Buses, trams and elevadores

City **Trams** and **buses** (daily 6am–midnight) are operated by the public transport company, Carris (☎213 613 000, ⓦ www.carris.pt). Buses (*autocarros*) run just about everywhere in the Lisbon area – the most useful ones are outlined in the box above.

Trams (*eléctricos*) run on five routes, which are marked on the chapter maps. Ascending some of the steepest urban gradients in the world, most are worth taking for the ride alone, especially the cross-city tram #28 (see p.76).

Sightseeing tours

Open-top bus tour The one-hour "Circuito Tejo" (hourly 9.15am–8.15pm; €14, ticket also valid on public transport) takes passengers around Lisbon's principal sights; a day-ticket allows you to get on and off whenever you want. The "Olisipo" tour departs three times daily to Parque das Nações (see p.136) for the same price. Both tours depart from Praça do Comércio. (Information ☎213 582 334, ⊛www.carristur.pt.)

Tourist tram tour The "Elétrico das Colinas" (Hills Tour) takes passengers on a ninety-minute ride in an early twentieth-century tram (hourly from 9am–6am; Nov–Feb three daily; €17), departing from Praça do Comércio and touring around Alfama, Chiado and São Bento. (Information on ☎213 582 334)

Art Shuttle Upmarket minibus service which can take 2–8 people on three-hour city tours for €35 (May–Sept). Reservations on ☎800 250 251, ⊛www.artshuttle.net.

River cruises Two-hour cruises along the Tejo depart from Praça do Comércio's Estação Fluvial (daily 11am & 3pm), stopping at Parque das Nações (11.45am & 3.45pm, though only when tides permit) and Belém (1pm & 5pm). The price (€20) includes a drink and commentary, and tickets are valid for returns on the later boats. Reservations on ☎218 820 348.

Walks Four themed two-hour guided walks are offered by Lisbon Walker (☎218 861 840, ⊛www.lisbonwalker.com; €15), departing from outside café Martinho da Arcada (see p.136) at 10am and 5pm.

Another picturesque route is taken by #12, which circles the castle area east of the city centre, via Largo Martim Moniz. Other useful routes are taken by the air-conditioned "supertram" #15 from Praça da Figueira to Belém (look for the sign Algés on the front), and #18, which runs from Rua da Alfândega via Praça do Comércio to the Palácio da Ajuda. The remaining route, #25, runs from Rua da Alfândega to Campo Ourique via Cais do Sodré, Lapa and Estrela (see p.66).

Also particular to Lisbon are the city's four *elevadores* – street lifts. These consist of three funicular railways offering quick access to the heights of the Bairro Alto (see p.90) and to the eastern side of Avenida da Liberdade (p.122); and one giant lift, the Elevador da Santa Justa (see p.53) which goes up to the foot of the Bairro Alto near Chiado.

The same tickets are valid on buses, trams and *elevadores* (though not on the metro or ferries), and can be bought either individually (€1.20 per ride) or in advance (€1.50, valid for two journeys) from kiosks in Praça do Comércio, Praça da Figueira and other bus terminals.

Tickets are validated by punching them into the machine next to the driver when you board. Note that the modern tram #15 has an automatic ticket machine on board and does not issue change. You can also load up a *Sete Colinas* card (see Tickets and travel passes above) with five units for €3.50 or ten for €6.50.

Taxis

Lisbon's cream taxis are inexpensive, with a minimum charge of €2 and an average ride running to €8–10. Fares are higher from 10pm to 6am, at weekends and on public holidays, when the minimum charge is €2.50. Bags in the boot incur a €0.60 fee. Taxis have meters, which should be switched on, and tips are not expected. Outside the rush hour taxis can be flagged down quite easily in the street or, alternatively, head for one of the ranks such as those outside the main train stations. At night, it's usually best to get a restaurant to phone a taxi for you (attracts an extra charge of €0.80), or try Rádio Taxis (☎218 119 000), Autocoope (☎217 932 756) or Teletáxi (☎218 111 100).

Local cuisine

At their finest, Portuguese dishes can be a revelation, made with fresh ingredients bursting with flavour. Grilled meats and fish tend to be the best bets, usually accompanied by rice or chips and salad. But unless you go upmarket, don't expect sophisticated sauces or delicate touches: stews, in particular, are not for the faint-hearted; offal features highly on most menus; and the ever-present *bacalhau* (dried salted cod) can be an acquired taste. Lisbon specialities include *santola recheado* (stuffed spider crabs) and *pastéis de nata* (custard tarts, best enjoyed with a *bica*, a wickedly powerful espresso coffee).

Lisbon has some of the best-value restaurants of any European city, many serving food in traditional interiors that have barely changed since the nineteenth century. A **set menu** (*ementa turística*) will get you a three-course meal for around €10–15 anywhere in the city, though you can eat for less by sticking to the ample main dishes or by choosing the daily specials – indeed, you may find the *meia doce* (half portion) sufficient for a main course. When you sit down, you will usually be presented with starters of olives, cheeses, spreads and sometimes cold meat or seafood. You'll be charged for anything you eat; if you don't take anything, make sure only the cover charge is on the bill.

Most Portuguese dine at around 8.30 or 9pm, so to guarantee the best table, turn up early or make sure you reserve in advance, especially on Friday or Saturday evenings. Telephone numbers for restaurants are given in the guide.

Festivals and events

The Portuguese have a reputation for being somewhat reserved, at least in comparison with their Spanish neighbours, but they know how to have a good time when it comes to festivals. Music and the arts are also highly valued and the year is punctuated by a series of cultural events that present concerts and exhibitions at venues across the city – the listings magazines *Follow me Lisboa* (in English) and *Agenda Cultural* (in Portuguese) have the best listings, or ask at the tourist office. The following is a rundown of the main events.

February–March
Carnival This festival has been revived recently with Brazilian-style parades and costumes, mainly at Parque das Nações.

March–April
Superbock Superrock Annual rock festival with local and international bands in various venues. (W www.superbock.pt).

May
Rock in Rio Biannual (even yearly) five-day rock festival (W www.rockinrio-lisboa.sapo.pt) in Parque Bela Vista (see p.132).

June
Festival Alkantara International contemporary arts festival, with dance, theatre, music and exhibitions throughout the city.

Santos Populares Street-partying to celebrate the saints' days – **António** (**June 13**), **João** (**June 24**) and **Pedro** (**June 29**). Celebrations for each begin on the evening before the actual day. The main festival is for **Santo António**, a public holiday when the whole city is decked out in coloured ribbons, with pots of lucky basil on every window sill.

There are festivals in each district on the evening of the 12th, with a main parade down Avenida da Liberdade. The best street party is in Alfama, with food and drinks stalls in just about every square. On June 13, the "Brides of Santo António" sees a collective wedding ceremony at the Igreja de Santo António. In Sintra, the main *festa* is for **São Pedro**, starting on June 28.

Gay pride The increasingly popular gay pride event (Arraial Pride) changes venues but has recently been held at Monsanto.

June–July

Handicrafts fair A state-run handicrafts fair, with live folk music, is held in Estoril on the Avenida de Portugal, near the Casino. A similar event occurs during the same period at FIL (ⓦ www.fil.pt), the main exhibition hall at the Parque das Nações, when international and Portuguese regional crafts are displayed and for sale.

The Sintra Music Festival This music festival sees performances by international orchestras, musicians and dance groups in parks, gardens and palaces in and around Sintra, Estoril and Cascais. Tickets and programmes for all performances are available from the Gabinete do Sintra-Festival, Praça da República 23, Sintra (ⓣ 219 243 518, ⓦ www.cm -sintra.pt). An offshoot of the festival is the "Noites de Bailado" held in the Centro Cultural Olga Cadaval near Sintra train station (ⓣ 219 107 118), a series of ballet, dance and operatic performances, again with top international names.

July Beer festival Castelo do São Jorge is decked out with handicrafts and food stalls with lots of ale, together with a recreated medieval market (ⓦ www .centralcervejas.pt).

July–August

Jazz Numa Noite de Verão Big annual (Jazz on a Summer Night) festival at the Gulbenkian's open-air amphitheatre (ⓦ www.musica.gulbenkian.pt). Cascais also hosts a jazz festival at this time.

September

Lisbon Marathon Attracts thousands of runners for the route across Ponte Vasco da Gama to the finish in Parque das Nações (ⓦ www.maratonclubeportugal .com).

November

São Martinho November 11 is celebrated by the traditional tasting of the year's wine drunk with hot chestnuts, in memory of Saint Martinho who shared his cape with a poor man.

December–January

Christmas The build-up to Christmas begins in early December with Europe's tallest Christmas tree adorning the centre of Praça da Comércio. Distinctive hooped *bolo-rei* (dried-fruit "king cake") appears in shops and *pastelarias*. Christmas Day itself – when many cafés are open – remains a family affair, with traditional midnight Mass celebrated on December 24, followed by a meal of *bacalhau*.

New Year's Eve The best place to head to on is Praça do Comércio, where fireworks light up the riverfront. There are similar firework displays at Cascais, and the Parque das Nações.

Public Holidays

Official holidays: January 1 New Year's Day; February or March Carnival; Good Friday; April 25 celebration of the 1974 revolution; May 1 Labour Day; June 10 Portugal Day and Camões Day; June 13 Santo António; August 15 Feast of the Assumption; October 5 Republic Day; November 1 All Saints' Day; December 1 Independence Day, celebrating independence from Spain in 1640; December 8 Immaculate Conception; December 24–25 Christmas.

Ethnic Lisbon

Over 120,000 people of African and Asian descent live in the Greater Lisbon area, most hailing originally from Portugal's former colonies – Cape Verde, Angola, Mozambique, Brazil, Goa and Macao. The first Africans arrived as slaves in the fifteenth century during Portugal's maritime explorations. The 1974 revolution and subsequent independence of the former colonies saw another wave of immigrants settle in the capital. Nowadays African and Brazilian culture permeate Lisbon life, influencing its music, food, television and street slang. Most Lisboetas are rightly proud of their cosmopolitan city although, inevitably, racism persists and few from ethnic minorities have managed to break through the glass ceiling to the top jobs.

Directory

Airlines Air France, Avda 5 de Outubro 206 ☎808 202 800; Air Luxor, Avda da República 101 ☎218 438 610; Alitalia, Praça Marquês de Pombal 1 5° ☎800 307 300; British Airways, Avda da Liberdade 36–2° ☎213 217 900; Iberia, Rua Barata Salgueiro 28–6 ☎213 110 600; KLM, Campo Grande 220h ☎217 055 010, Lufthansa, aeroporto ☎214 245 155; TAP, Pr. Marquês de Pombal 15 ☎707 205 700.

American Express The local agent is Top Tours, Avda Duque de Loulé 108 ☎213 155 885; Mon–Fri 9.30am–1pm & 2.30–6.30pm.

Banks and Exchange Usual bank opening hours are Monday to Friday 8.30am to 3pm. Most main branches are located in the Baixa district and are equipped with automatic exchange machines for various currencies and denominations. Changing cash in banks is easy, too, and shouldn't attract more than €3 commission, though not all banks offer an exchange service. By far the easiest way to get money in Portugal is to use your debit or credit card

Lisbon on the Internet

Specific websites are given in the text. The following are useful general sites on Lisbon and around.

ⓦ**www.cm-lisboa.pt/turismo** Good for details on upcoming events, this is the Lisbon town hall's site.

ⓦ**www.ipmuseus.pt** The Institute for Portuguese Museums site, with links to all the country's main museums.

ⓦ**www.portugalvirtual.pt** Comprehensive directory of everything Portuguese – from hotels to shops, tourist sites to businesses.

ⓦ**www.portuguesewine.com** A rundown of the best ports and madeiras, and reviews of the different wine-producing regions of Portugal.

ⓦ**www.visitlisboa.com/atl-turismolisboa.pt/askmelisboa.com** The Lisbon Welcome Centre's comprehensive sites, with details (in English) of hotels, restaurants, news and events, and answers to frequently asked questions.

ⓦ**www.visitportugal.com** The official Portuguese website, run by ICEP (Investments, Trade and Tourism of Portugal), with information about various tourist attractions and some practical advice.

to withdraw cash from any of the large number of ATM machines, called "Multibanco". You'll find them all over Lisbon and you can withdraw up to €200 per day, though check fees with your personal bank.

Buses The main terminal is at Sete Rios (see map p.142). Other bus services to Caparica, Sesimbra, Setúbal and places south of the Tejo leave from Praça de Espanha (metro Praça de Espanha ☎217 262 740, ⊛www.tsuldotejo.pt).

Car Rental Alamo/Guerin, Avda Alvares Cabral 45b ☎213 703 400; Auto Jardim, Rua Luciano Cordeiro 6 ☎213 549 182, airport ☎218 463 187; Avis, Campo Grande 390 ☎217 547 800; Budget, Rua Castilho 167b ☎213 860 516, airport ☎218 478 803; Europcar, Av. António Augusto Aguiar 24 ☎213 535 115, airport ☎218 401 176; Hertz, Rua Castilho 72 ☎213 812 430, airport ☎218 463 154; Nova Rent, Largo Monterroio Mascarenhas 9 ☎213 845 270.

Churches Most churches are free to enter and are open daily; feel free to walk in and look around, but remember to be respectful and dress appropriately.

Cinemas Lisbon has dozens of cinemas, virtually all of them showing original-language films with Portuguese subtitles, and ticket prices are low (around €6; cheaper on Mondays). The tourist offices should be able to tell you what's on, or consult the listings outside the ABEP kiosk on the southeast corner of Praça dos Restauradores. Most cinemas are open from around midday, with last performances at around 11pm. Among the most interesting arthouse venues is Quarteto, Rua das Flores Lima 1 (☎217 971 244; metro Entre Campos), off Avenida Estados Unidos, with four screens. The Instituto da Cinemateca Portuguesa, Rua Barata Salgueiro (☎213 596 266 ⊛www.cinemateca.pt; metro Avenida), the national film theatre, has twice-daily shows, ranging from contemporary Portuguese films to silent classics, and contains its own cinema museum.

Mainstream movies are shown at various multiplexes around the city. The best and most central is the São Jorge, Avenida da Liberdade 175 (☎213 103 400), with three large screens.

Disabled Travellers Lisbon airport offers a service for wheelchair-users if advance notice is given (☎213 632 044), while the Orange Badge symbol is recognized for disabled car parking. The main public transport company, Carris,

offers an inexpensive dial-a-ride minibus service, O Serviço Especial de Transporte de Deficientes (€1.20 per trip; Mon–Fri 6.30am–10pm, Sat & Sun 8am–10pm; ☎213 613 141, ⊛www.carris.pt), though two days' advance notice and a medical certificate are required.

Electricity Portugal uses two-pin plugs (220v). UK appliances will work with a continental adaptor.

Embassies and consulates Australia, Avda da Liberdade 196–2°, metro Avenida; ☎213 101 500; Canada, Avda da Liberdade 196–200, metro Avenida; ☎213 164 600; Ireland, Rua da Imprensa à Estrela 1–4°, tram #28 to Estrela; ☎213 929 440; New Zealand, Avda António Aguiar 122, metro São Sebastião or Parque; ☎213 509 690; South Africa, Avda Luís Bivar 10, metro Picoas; ☎213 192 200; UK, Rua de São Bernardo 33, metro Rato; ☎213 924 000; USA, Avda das Forças Armadas, metro Jardim Zoológico; ☎217 273 300.

Emergencies Call ☎112 for police, ambulance and fire.

Gay and lesbian Lisbon's gay and lesbian scene is becoming more open in a city that was, until recently, fairly conservative. The Centro Comunitário Gay e Lésbico de Lisboa at Rua de São Lázaro 88 (☎218 873 918; Wed–Thurs 6pm–11pm, Fri & Sat 6pm–1am) is Lisbon's main gay and lesbian community centre just north of Metro Martim Moniz, with its own café. The centre organizes events and is happy to give details of gay-friendly venues. It is run by ILGA whose comprehensive website (⊛www.ilga-portugal.org) is in English and Portuguese.

Hospitals The privately run British Hospital, Rua Saraiva de Carvalho 49 (☎213 955 067), has English-speaking staff and doctors on call 8.30am–9pm. There are various other public hospitals around the city.

Internet access There are lots of Internet points and cyber-cafés charging around €1–3 per hour for Internet use. Useful options in each main neighbourhood include: Ponto Net, above the Lisbon Welcome Centre in Praça do Comércio, Baixa (daily 9am–8pm; ☎210 312 815); Web Café, Rua do Diário de Notícias 16, Bairro Alto (daily 4pm–2am; ☎213 421 181); and Cyberica, Rua Duques de Bragança 7, Chiado (daily 11am–midnight; ☎213 421 707).

Left luggage There are 24hr lockers at the airport, the main train stations and the bus stations, charging €2–7, depending on the size of the bag.

Lost property Report any loss to the tourist police station in the Foz Cultura building in Palácio Foz, Praça dos Restauradores (daily 24hr ☎213 421 634). For items left on public transport, contact Carris ☎218 535 403.

Mail Post offices (*correios*) are normally open Monday to Friday 8.30am to 6.30pm. The main Lisbon office is at Praça dos Restauradores 58 (☎213 238 700) (see map p.58–59). Stamps (*selos*) are sold at post offices and anywhere that has the sign "Correio de Portugal – Selos" displayed.

Money Portugal's currency is the euro (€), with notes issued in denominations of 5, 10, 20, 50, 100, 200 and 500 euros, and coins in denominations of 1, 2, 5, 10, 20 and 50 cents, and 1 and 2 euros.

Pharmacies Pharmacies, which are the first point of call for most ill people in Portugal, are open Mon–Fri 9am–1pm & 3–7pm, Sat 9am–1pm. Local papers carry information about 24hr pharmacies and the details are posted on every pharmacy door, or call ☎118.

Sports Even before the Euro 2004 championships, Lisboetas have always had a passion for football, and the city boasts two of Europe's top sides, Benfica and Sporting (fixtures at ✪www.portuguese soccer.com). The Lisbon area also contains some of Europe's best golf courses (info at ✪www. portugalgolf.pt), and Atlantic beaches that are ideal for surfing and windsurfing. Horse-riding is superb in the Sintra hills, and skilled horsemanship can also be seen at Portuguese bullfights, which are less bloody than their Spanish counterpart. The Lisbon marathon in November and April's Estoril tennis Open draw international athletes to the city.

Telephones Calls are easily made using card-operated public telephones called *credifones*, which you'll find all over Lisbon. Phone cards cost either €3, €6 or €9, and are available from post offices, larger newsagents and street kiosks. Calls can also be made from the telephone office (Mon–Fri 8am–11pm) next to the main post office in Praça dos Restauradores. Most European-subscribed mobile phones will work in Lisbon, though you are likely to be charged extra for incoming and outgoing calls. The cheap rate for national and international calls is applicable between 9pm and 9am Monday to Friday, and all day weekends and public holidays.

Tickets You can buy tickets for Lisbon's cinemas, theatres and many concerts from the ABEP Kiosk (*Agencia de Bilhetes para Espectaculos Públicos*), on Praça dos Restauradores (daily 9am–9.30pm; see Rossio map p.58–59); the ticket desk in FNAC in the Armazéns do Chiado shopping centre (see p.85); Valentim de Carvalho on Rua do Carmo 28, as well as from the main venues themselves. Online tickets can be purchased from ✪www.ticketline.pt.

Time Portuguese time is the same as Greenwich Mean Time (GMT). Clocks go forward an hour in late March and back to GMT in late October.

Tipping Service charges are included in hotel and restaurant bills. It's usual to round up restaurant bills to the nearest €1 or so; other than this, tips are not expected. Hotel porters, toilet attendants and cinema ushers do expect tips of at least €0.50 though.

Toilets There are very few public toilets in the streets, although they can be found in nearly all the museums and main tourist sights (signed variously as *casa de banho, retrete, banheiro, lavabos* or "WC"), and it is not that difficult to sneak into a café or restaurant if need be. Gents are usually marked "H" (*homens*) or "C" (*cabalheiros*), and ladies "M" (*mulheres*) or "S" (*senhoras*).

Travel agents Marcus & Harting, Rossio 45–50 (☎213 224 550), is a good, central option for bus tickets and general travel information. The well-informed Top Tours, Avda Duque de Loulé 108 (☎213 108 800), near metro Marquês de Pombal, also acts as an American Express agent. USIT Tagus, Rua Camilo Castelo Branco 20 (☎213 525 986), specializes in discounted student tickets and sells ISIC cards.

Water Lisbon's water is technically safe to drink, though you may prefer bottled water. Inexpensive bottled water is sold by any food store or supermarket.

Chronology

Chronology

60 BC ▶ Julius Caesar establishes Olisipo as the capital of the Roman Empire's western colony.

711 ▶ Moors from North Africa conquer Iberia, building a fortress by the *alhama* (hot springs), now known as Alfama.

1147 ▶ Afonso Henriques, the first king of the newly established Portuguese state, retakes Lisbon from the Moors and builds a cathedral on the site of the former mosque.

1495–1521 ▶ The reign of Dom Manuel I coincides with the golden age of the Portuguese discoveries. So-called "Manueline" architecture celebrates the opening of sea routes.

1498 ▶ Vasco da Gama returns to Belém with spices from India, the profit from which partly funds the building of the elaborate monastery of Jeronimos in Belém.

1706–50 ▶ During the reign of Dom João V, gold and diamonds from the Portuguese colony Brazil kick-start a second golden age, which is reflected in opulent Baroque architecture, such as the palace at Queluz.

1755 ▶ The Great Earthquake flattens much of Lisbon. The Baixa is hurriedly rebuilt in "Pombaline" style, named after the Marquês de Pombal.

1800s ▶ Maria II (1843–53) holds the throne with German consort, Fernando II, and establishes the elaborate palaces at Ajuda and Pena in Sintra. Fado becomes popular in the Alfama. Avenida da Liberdade is laid out to form a new city axis.

1900–10 ▶ Carlos I is assassinated in Lisbon in 1908, while two years later, the exile of Manuel II marks the end of the Portuguese monarchy and birth of the Republic.

1932–68 ▶ Salazar's dictatorship sees development stagnate. Despite massive rural poverty, elaborate "New State" architecture includes the impressive Ponte 25 de Abril, originally named Ponte de Salazar.

1974 ▶ April 25 marks a largely peaceful Revolution. Former Portuguese colonies are granted independence, leading to massive immigration, mainly from Mozambique and Angola.

1986 ▶ Entry to the European Community enables a rapid road-building programme and redevelopment of Lisbon.

1990s ▶ Lisbon's role as Capital of Culture (1994) and host of Expo 98 attracts substantial investment, funding new roads, an extension of the metro, the Ponte Vasco da Gama and the establishment of the Parque das Nações. Many of the new buildings are showcases for top architects.

2000–10 ▶ Lisbon hosts the finals of the European Football Championships 2004 in two brand new soccer stadia. The international popularity of fado singer Mariza opens up the Portuguese music form to a global audience.

Language

The basics

English is widely spoken in most of Lisbon's hotels and tourist restaurants, but you will find a few words of Portuguese extremely useful if you are travelling on public transport, or in more out of the way places. If you have some knowledge of Spanish, you won't have much problem reading Portuguese. Understanding it when it's spoken, though, is a different matter: pronunciation is entirely different and at first even the easiest words are hard to distinguish. Once you've started to figure out the words it gets a lot easier very quickly.

Pronunciation

The chief difficulty with **pronunciation** is the lack of clarity of the language – consonants tend to be slurred, vowels nasal and often ignored altogether. The **consonants** are, at least, consistent:

C is soft before E and I, hard otherwise unless it has a cedilla – *açucar* (sugar) is pronounced "assookar".

CH is somewhat softer than in English; *chá* (tea) sounds like Shah.

J is pronounced like the "s" in pleasure, as is G except when it comes before a "hard" vowel (A, O and U).

LH sounds like "lyuh" (Alcantarilha).

Q is always pronounced as a "k".

S before a consonant or at the end of a word becomes "sh", otherwise it's as in English – Sagres is pronounced "Sahgresh".

X is also pronounced "sh" - caixa (cash desk) is pronounced "kaisha".

Vowels are worse – flat and truncated, they're often difficult for English-speaking tongues to get around. The only way to learn is to listen: accents Ã, Õ or É turn them into longer, more familiar sounds. When two vowels come together they continue to be enunciated separately except in the case of **EI** and **OU** – which sound like A and long O respectively. E at the end of a word is silent unless it has an accent, so that *carne* (meat) is pronounced "karn", while café sounds much as you'd expect. The **tilde over Ã or Õ** renders the pronunciation much like the French -an and -on endings only more nasal. More common is **ÃO** (as in *pão*, bread – *são*, saint – *limão*, lemon), which sounds something like a strangled yelp of "Ow!" cut off in midstream.

Words and phrases

Basics			
sim; não	yes; no	adeus, até logo	goodbye, see you later
olá; bom dia	hello; good morning	hoje; amanhã	today; tomorrow
boa tarde/noite	good afternoon/night	por favor/se faz favor	please

LANGUAGE

Words and phrases

tudo bem?	everything all right?
está bem	it's all right/OK
obrigado/a	thank you (male/ female speaker)
onde; que	where; what
quando; porquê	when; why
como; quanto	how; how much
não sei	I don't know
sabe…?	do you know…?
pode…?	could you…?
há…? (silent "H")	is there…? there is
tem…? (pronounced *taying*)	do you have…?
queria…	I'd like…
desculpe; com licença	sorry; excuse me
fala Inglês?	do you speak English?
não compreendo	I don't understand
este/a; esse/a	this; that
agora; mais tarde	now; later
mais; menos	more; less
grande; pequeno	big; little
aberto; fechado	open; closed
senhoras; homens	women; men
lavabo/quarto de banho	toilet/bathroom

Getting around

esquerda, direita, sempre em frente	left, right, straight ahead
aqui; ali	here; there
perto; longe	near; far
Onde é a estação de camionetas?	Where is the bus station?
a paragem de autocarro para…	the bus stop for…
Donde parte o autocarro para…?	Where does the bus to…leave from
A que horas parte? (chega a…?)	What time does it leave? (arrive at…?)
Pare aqui por favor	Stop here please
bilhete (para)	ticket (to)
ida e volta	round trip

Accommodation

Queria um quarto	I'd like a room
É para uma noite (semana)	It's for one night (week)
É para uma pessoa (duas pessoas)	It's for one person/ two people
Quanto custa?	How much is it?
Posso ver?	May I see/ look around?
Há um quarto mais barato?	Is there a cheaper room?
com duche	with a shower

Shopping

Quanto é?	How much is it?
banco; câmbio	bank; change
correios	post office
(dois) selos	(two) stamps
Como se diz isto em Português?	What's this called in Portuguese?
O que é isso?	What's that?

Days of the week

domingo	Sunday
segunda-feira	Monday
terça-feira	Tuesday
quarta-feira	Wednesday
quinta-feira	Thursday
sexta-feira	Friday
sábado	Saturday

Months

janeiro	January
fevereiro	February
março	March
abril	April
maio	May
junho	June
julho	July
agosto	August
setembro	September
outubro	October
novembro	November
dezembro	December

Numbers

um/uma	1
dois/duas	2
três	3
quatro	4
cinco	5
seis	6
sete	7
oito	8
nove	9
dez	10
onze	11

doze	12
treze	13
catorze	14
quinze	15
dezasseis	16
dezassete	17
dezoito	18
dezanove	19
vinte	20
vinte e um	21
trinta	30
quarenta	40
cinquenta	50
sessenta	60
setenta	70
oitenta	80
noventa	90
cem	100
cento e um	101
duzentos	200

quinhentos	500
mil	1000

Common signs

aberto	open
fechado	closed
hoje	today
amanha	tomorrow
saldo	sale
esgotado	sold out
entrada	entrance
saída	exit
puxe	pull
empurre	push
elevador	lift
pré-pagamento	pay in advance
perigo/perigoso	danger/ous
proibido estacionar	no parking
obras	(road) works

LANGUAGE Words and phrases

Menu glossary

Basic words and terms

assado	roasted
colher	spoon
conta	bill
copo	glass
cozido	boiled
ementa	menu
estrelado/frito	fried
faca	knife
fumado	smoked
garfo	fork
garrafa	bottle
grelhado	grilled
mexido	scrambled

Menu terms

pequeno almoço	breakfast
almoço	lunch
jantar	dinner
ementa turística	set menu of the day
prato do dia	dish of the day
especialidades	speciality
lista de vinhos	wine list
entradas	starters
petiscos	snacks
sobremesa	dessert

Soups, salad and staples

açorda	bread-based stew (often seafood)
açucár	sugar
arroz	rice
azeitonas	olives
batatas fritas	chips/french fries
caldo verde	cabbage soup
fruta	fruit
gaspacho	chilled vegetable soup
legumes	vegetables
massa	pasta
manteiga	butter
migas	meat or fish in a bready garlic sauce
molho (de tomate/ piri-piri)	tomato/chilli sauce
omeleta	omelette
ovos	eggs
pão	bread
pimenta	pepper
piri-piri	chilli sauce
queijo	cheese
sal	salt
salada	salad
sopa de legumes	vegetable soup
sopa de marisco	shellfish soup
sopa de peixe	fish soup

Fish and shellfish

arroz de marisco	seafood rice
atum	tuna
bacalhau à brás	salted cod with egg and potatoes
caldeirada	fish stew
camarões	shrimp
carapau	mackerel
cataplana	fish, shellfish or meat stewed in a circular metal dish
cherne	stone bass
dourada	bream
espada	scabbard fish
espadarte	swordfish
gambas	prawns
lagosta	lobster
lulas (grelhadas)	squid (grilled)
mexilhões	mussels
pescada	hake
polvo	octopus
robalo	sea bass
salmão	salmon
salmonete	red mullet
santola	spider crab
sapateira	crab
sardinhas na brasa	charcoal-grilled sardines
tamboril	monkfish
truta	trout
viera	scallop

Meat

alheira	chicken sausage
bife à portuguesa	thin beef steak with a fried egg on top
borrego	lamb
chanfana	lamb or goat casserole
chouriço	spicy sausage
coelho	rabbit
cordeiro	lamb

cozido à portuguesa	boiled casserole of meats and beans, served with rice and vegetables
dobrada/tripa	tripe
espetada mista	mixed meat kebab
febras	pork steaks
fiambre	ham
fígado	liver
frango no churrasco	barbecued chicken
leitão	roast suckling pig
pato	duck
perdiz	partridge
perú	turkey
picanha	strips of beef in garlic sauce
porco à alentejana	pork cooked with clams
presunto	smoked ham
rim	kidney
rodízio	variety of barbecued meats
rojões	cubed pork cooked in blood and potatoes
vitela	veal

Drinks

um copo/uma garrafa de/da...	a glass/bottle of...
vinho branco/tinto	white/red wine
cerveja	beer
água (sem/com gás)	mineral water (without/with gas)
fresca/natural	chilled/room temperature
sumo de laranja/ maçã	orange/apple juice
chá	tea
café	coffee
sem/com leite	without/with milk
sem/com açúcar	without/with sugar

Travel store

Available from all good bookstores D: Rough Guide DIRECTIONS

Kenya
Marrakesh **D**
Morocco
South Africa,
   Lesotho &
   Swaziland
Syria
Tanzania
Tunisia
West Africa
Zanzibar

Travel Specials
First-Time
   Around the
   World
First-Time Asia
First-Time
   Europe
First-Time Latin
   America
Travel Online
Travel Health
Travel Survival
Walks in London
   & SE England
Women Travel

Maps
Algarve
Amsterdam
Andalucia &
   Costa del Sol
Argentina
Athens
Australia
Barcelona
Berlin
Boston
Brittany
Brussels
California
Chicago
Corsica
Costa Rica &
   Panama
Crete
Croatia
Cuba
Cyprus
Czech Republic
Dominican
   Republic
Dubai & UAE
Dublin
Egypt
Florence & Siena
Florida

France
Frankfurt
Germany
Greece
Guatemala &
   Belize
Hong Kong
Iceland
Ireland
Kenya &
   Northern
   Tanzania
Lisbon
London
Los Angeles
Madrid
Mallorca
Malaysia
Marrakesh
Mexico
Miami & Key
   West
Morocco
New England
New York City
New Zealand
Northern Spain
Paris
Peru
Portugal
Prague
The Pyrenees
Rome
San Francisco
Sicily
South Africa
South India
Spain & Portugal
Sri Lanka
Tenerife
Thailand
Toronto
Trinidad &
   Tobago
Tuscany
Venice
Vietnam, Laos &
   Cambodia
Washington DC
Yucatán
   Peninsula

**Dictionary
Phrasebooks**
Croatian
Czech
Dutch
Egyptian Arabic

French
German
Greek
Hindi & Urdu
Italian
Japanese
Latin American
   Spanish
Mandarin
   Chinese
Mexican Spanish
Polish
Portuguese
Russian
Spanish
Swahili
Thai
Turkish
Vietnamese

Computers
Blogging
iPods, iTunes &
   music online
The Internet
Macs & OS X
PCs and Windows
PlayStation
   Portable (PSP)
Website Directory

Film & TV
American
   Independent
   Film
British Cult
   Comedy
Chick Flicks
Comedy Movies
Cult Movies
Gangster Movies
Horror Movies
Kids' Movies
Sci-Fi Movies
Westerns

Lifestyle
Babies
eBay
Ethical Shopping
Pregnancy
   & Birth

Music Guides
The Beatles
Bob Dylan
Book of Playlists
Classical Music
Elvis
Frank Sinatra
Heavy Metal
Hip-Hop
Jazz
Opera
Pink Floyd
Punk
Reggae
Rock
The Rolling
   Stones
Soul and R&B
World Music
(2 vols)

Popular Culture
Books for
   Teenagers
Children's Books,
   5-11
Conspiracy
   Theories
Cult Fiction
The Da Vinci
   Code
Lord of the Rings
Shakespeare
Superheroes
Unexplained
   Phenomena

Sport
Arsenal 11s
Celtic 11s
Chelsea 11s
Liverpool 11s
Man United 11s
Newcastle 11s
Rangers 11s
Tottenham 11s
Poker

Science
Climate Change
The Universe
Weather

For more information go to www.roughguides.com

Visit us online
www.roughguides.com

Information on over 25,000 destinations around the world

- **Read** Rough Guides' trusted travel info

- **Access** exclusive articles from Rough Guides authors

- **Update** yourself on new books, maps, CDs and other products

- **Enter** our competitions and win travel prizes

- **Share** ideas, journals, photos & travel advice with other users

- **Earn** points every time you contribute to the Rough Guide

  community and get rewards

BROADEN YOUR HORIZONS

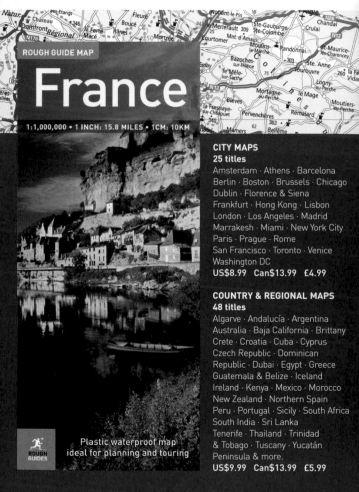

Rough Guide Music Titles

The Beatles • Bob Dylan • Classical Music
Elvis • Frank Sinatra • Heavy Metal • Hip-Hop
iPods, iTunes & music online • Jazz
Book of Playlists • Opera • Pink Floyd • Punk
Reggae • Rock • The Rolling Stones
Soul and R&B • World Music Vol 1 & 2

BROADEN YOUR HORIZONS

A Rough Guide to Rough Guides

In 1981, Mark Ellingham, a recent graduate in English from Bristol University, was travelling in Greece on a tiny budget and couldn't find the right guidebook. With a group of friends he wrote his own guide, combining a contemporary, journalistic style with a practical approach to travellers' needs. That first Rough Guide was a student scheme that became a publishing phenomenon. Today, Rough Guides include recommendations from shoestring to luxury and cover hundreds of destinations around the globe, including almost every country in the Americas and Europe, more than half of Africa and most of Asia and Australasia. Millions of readers relish Rough Guides' wit and inquisitiveness as much as their enthusiastic, critical approach and value-for-money ethos. The guides' ever-growing team of authors and photographers is spread all over the world.

In the early 1990s, Rough Guides branched out of travel, with the publication of Rough Guides to World Music, Classical Music and the Internet. All three have become benchmark titles in their fields, spearheading the publication of a range of more than 350 titles under the Rough Guide name, including phrasebooks, waterproof maps, music guides from Opera to Heavy Metal, reference works as diverse as Conspiracy Theories and Shakespeare, and popular culture books from iPods to Poker. Rough Guides also produce a series of more than 120 World Music CDs in partnership with World Music Network.

Visit www.roughguides.com to see our latest publications.

Rough Guide travel images are available for commercial licensing at www.roughguidespictures.com

Publishing information

This second edition published March 2007 by Rough Guides Ltd, 80 Strand, London WC2R 0RL; 345 Hudson St, 4th Floor, New York, NY 10014, USA.

Distributed by the Penguin Group
Penguin Books Ltd, 80 Strand, London WC2R 0RL
Penguin Group (USA), 375 Hudson St, NY 10014, USA
14 Local Shopping Centre, Panchsheel Park, New Delhi 110017, India
Penguin Group (Australia), 250 Camberwell Rd, Camberwell, Victoria 3124, Australia
Penguin Group (Canada), 10 Alcorn Ave, Toronto, ON M4V 1E4, Canada
Penguin Group (NZ), 67 Apollo Drive, Mairangi Bay, Auckland 1310, New Zealand

Typeset in Bembo and Helvetica to an original design by Henry Iles.

Cover concept by Peter Dyer

Printed and bound in China

© Matthew Hancock 2007

No part of this book may be reproduced in any form without permission from the publisher except for the quotation of brief passages in reviews.

212pp includes index

A catalogue record for this book is available from the British Library

ISBN 13: 978-1-84353-739-7

The publishers and authors have done their best to ensure the accuracy and currency of all the information in Lisbon DIRECTIONS, however, they can accept no responsibility for any loss, injury, or inconvenience sustained by any traveller as a result of information or advice contained in the guide.

5   7   9   8   6   4

Help us update

We've gone to a lot of effort to ensure that the second edition of Lisbon DIRECTIONS is accurate and up to date. However, things change – places get "discovered", opening hours are notoriously fickle, restaurants and rooms raise prices or lower standards. If you feel we've got it wrong or left something out, we'd like to know, and if you can remember the address, the price, the phone number, so much the better.

We'll credit all contributions, and send a copy of the next edition (or any other DIRECTIONS guide or Rough Guide if you prefer) for the best letters. Everyone who writes to us and isn't already a subscriber will receive a copy of our full-colour thrice-yearly newsletter. Please mark letters: "Lisbon DIRECTIONS Update" and send to: Rough Guides, 80 Strand, London WC2R 0RL, or Rough Guides, 4th Floor, 345 Hudson St, New York, NY 10014. Or send an email to mail@roughguides.com

Have your questions answered and tell others about your trip at www.roughguides.atinfopop.com

Rough Guide credits

Text editor: Lucy White
Layout: Umesh Aggarwal
Photography: Demetrio Carrasco
Cartography: Jasbir Sandhu

Picture editor: Mark Thomas
Proofreaders: Stewart Wild and Diane Margolis
Production: Aimee Hampson
Cover design: Chlöe Roberts

SMALL PRINT

The author

Matthew Hancock fell in love with Portugal and its people when he was a teacher in Lisbon. He later returned to the country to walk the 775-mile long Portuguese-Spanish border. Now a journalist and editor living in Dorset, he is also the author of the Rough Guides to Algarve and Madeira and co-author of the Rough Guide to Portugal.

Acknowledgement

Thanks to Joe Budd for nightlife and Amanda Tomlin, Alex and Olivia for ideas and support. Also Júlio Pires and Manuel Cabral Morais (members of ILGA Portugal); Vítor Carriço at the Lisbon Tourist Board; Carlos Oliveira at ICEP; Luke and Paula for their usual assistance; everyone who helped me with accommodation; and the staff at Rough Guides, especially Lucy White for her patient editing; Mark Thomas for picture research; Demetrio Carrasco for photography; Jasbir Sandhu for maps and Stewart Wild and Diane Margolis for proofreading

Readers' letters

Louise Boulton, Julie Craig, Akane and Paul Davis, Marjorie De'ath, Suzanne E Harvey, Reem Khokar, Paul Killingbeck, Pierre Moret, Richard Rafeek, Margaret Ross, Adam Rothapel and Isobel Pearce, Ann Sargent, Susan Saxton, Mick Shkrapnell, Theo Smit, Joel Wallace

Photo credits

All photos © Rough Guides except the following

Introduction
p.1 Bairro Alto house © Matthew Hancock
p.7 Café in Chiado © Matthew Hancock
p.7 Alfama © Matthew Hancock
p.8 Cyclists in Parque das Naçoes © Matthew Hancock

Ideas
p.23 Palácio Marquêses de Fronteira © Massimo Listri/Corbis
p.25 Ajuda, Banqueting hall © Alain I e Garsmeur/Corbis
p.30 Convento dos Capuchos © Charles dos Capuchos/Corbis

p.31 The initiation well © Bo Zanders/Corbis
p.32 Orion Eden, rooftop pool © Patricia Nogueira/ VIP Hotels
p.44 Puppet Museum © Pedro Nereu/Museu de Marioneta
p.45 Dolphins at Arrábida © Matthew Hancock
p.47 View of Arrábida © Matthew Hancock

Places
p.140 Parque das Naçoes © Matthew Hancock
p.157 Estoril Beach © Ken Welsh/Alamy
p.163 Surfer © Peter Domotor/Alamy

Selected images from our guidebooks are available for licensing from:
ROUGHGUIDESPICTURES.COM

Index

Maps are marked in colour

WHEREVER YOU ARE,

WHEREVER YOU'RE GOING

WE'VE GOT YOU COVERED!

Rough Guides Travel Insurance

Visit our website at www.roughguides.com/insurance or call:

📞 UK: 0800 083 9507

📞 Spain: 900 997 149

📞 Australia: 1300 669 999

📞 New Zealand: 0800 55 99 11

📞 Worldwide: +44 870 890 2843

📞 USA, call toll free on: 1 800 749 4922

Please quote our ref: *Rough Guides books*

Cover for over 46 different nationalities and available in 4 different languages.